You Mean, There's

# GENIUS

in My Hip Hop?

The Complete Guide to Understanding Underground HipHopology

## Dr. F.W. Gooding, Jr.

*The Author:* Dr. F.W. Gooding Jr., is a recovering attorney who decided to pursue his passion of questing for justice around the classroom rather than inside the courtroom. Laden with a Ph.D. in History from Georgetown University, Dr. Gooding spends his spare time as an Ethnic Studies Professor at Northern Arizona University.

This title is published by On the Reelz Press
899 W. Weston Trail, Suite Mt. Humphreys, Flagstaff, Arizona, 86005, USA.

On the Reelz Press, and the On the Reelz Press logo are trademarks of
On the Reelz Press, Inc. The Minority Reporter, and The Minority Reporter logo
are trademarks of On the Reelz Press, Inc.
*www.otrpress.com*


ISBN: 978-0-9778048-5-6
Printed in the United States of America.

On the Reelz Press books may be purchased for educational, business, or personal use. For more information, contact On the Reelz Press corporate/institutional sales department at (202) 288-5562 or at otrpressinfo@gmail.com.

Special thanks to Ms. Wall and her undying love for the magic of music...
and of course ous to our #1 fan . . .

# DEDICATION

To the dedicated

Racism:
laugh

or cry

# TABLE OF CONTENTS

This
text
borrows
liberally
from
concepts
expounded
upon
in
more
detail
in
You Mean, There's RACE in My Movie?
(cited herein as YMTRIMM)
also
available
at
www.otrpress.com.

# Zero

# INTRODUCTION

### What is so GENIUS about Hip Hop?

# CREATIVE GENIUS

Quite simply, our operating definition of **GENIUS** is **"the ability to generate and create that which is particularly intelligent, insightful or inspirational."** The locus of our working definition is rooted in the ability to channel creative forces for a greater purpose. Creative forces are vital to life since destructive forces are ever present (e.g., our bodies specifically fight decay on a daily basis). Thus, if creation is the opposite of destruction, then **GENIUS** within us all represents the innate ability to seek, find and fight for that which is best in life. **GENIUS** is survival of the highest order.

Hip Hop is no different.

Hip Hop is more than just a song or a genre; it is a loosely organized culture oriented in a way of being that depends upon creativity as its sustaining life force. For the uninitiated, perhaps all Hip Hop "sounds the same." Sure. But if one knows where to look (or listen rather), they will find so much more than what they bargained for — which is partly the reason why we are here — to explore the nuances and contours of this cultural philosophy and what makes it so inspirational, or **GENIUS**.

# BUT GENIUS YOU SAY?

Many a word has been spoken, written or typed to describe the phenomena and force that is Hip Hop.[1] Confusing to some, captivating to many, Hip Hop has forever been within the crosswinds of controversy. People continue to argue about what it is, what it means, or what is the true extent of its effect. Fine. What remains clear is that Hip Hop as it is has changed the world as it were.[2]

Forever.

Even if Hip Hop were to die tomorrow[3] (unlikely), the indisputable fact remains indisputable — that Hip Hop, with its dynamic sound, engaging look and penetrating ethos, has permanently ensconced itself within mainstream culture, having grown into a multi-billion dollar cultural *tour de force* of global proportion.[4] No matter how society or culture will adapt over time in the future, Hip Hop's position as noteworthy and memorable within human history is secure.[5]

Despite blossoming into an international phenomena where the greatest breakdancers today are rumored never to have left the borders of China, Hip Hop claims its beginnings from rather humble beginnings. Poor black and brown peoples silenced, forgotten, disenfranchised and disconnected from the sprawling, burgeoning metropolitan monstrosity called New York City used innate powers of creativity to raise their voices and in turn raise the consciousness of anyone who would listen and acknowledge their existence.

This creative force, hewn and sewn together with the rudimentary tools of "two turn tables and a mic,"[6] arrived with a big bang indeed, constantly combusting with all of its accents and anomalies, its gifts and limitations, its critiques and inconsistencies. Well, this creative force can be called nothing shy of **GENIUS**. And so our business here. As said before, much has been written about Hip Hop already. Some materials about Hip Hop are enlightening while others are too esoteric and **WACK** (sorry, we are going to follow a Hip Hop tenement and "keep it real" here; time is of the essence).

Hence, what we aim to do within these pages is not repeat, recycle or "remix" what has already been said about Hip Hop's origins. But rather, we seek to understand Hip Hop's originality and the nuanced ways in which it articulates its loose, yet complex conceptual framework, or *Hiphopology*. Quite simply, Hip Hop is now developed enough where we seriously have to take it seriously. Thus, as with any other subject worthy of solemn contemplation, we need to consistently study it to appreciate it even further and provide a clear roadmap for future aficionados who will inevitably want to know more.

Of course, we shall elaborate over the course of the next few pages but in short, Hip Hop is **GENIUS** precisely because it moves our bodies, minds and souls. When something has the power to cheer you up on a bad day, motivate you to get out of bed, get you "hype," or pumped up while exercising, help you understand and cope with institutional or social pressures that you endure, or get you excited to dance like a raving lunatic with total strangers at a house party or crowded club, then naturally you may seek to understand this force.

# BOOK FORMAT

At **On the Reelz Press,** we believe the most precious resource of all is time, ergo time is always of the essence. Our specialty-crafted Modus Operandi or M.O. is to therefore get **2 tha Point** with **FullProof Analysis**, then step out the way before you **Just Add Water** to see your understanding grow.

## 2 tha Point

Since time is of the essence, we seek to unburden our readers with only 10 chapters of only 10 pages of content or less.

## FullProof

What makes our content virtually foolproof is that we are literally full of proof, as in, we provide at least 10 examples/references or more for each core chapter (e.g., Chapters 3 - 8). This pragmatic approach underscores our strong preference for careful observation rather than careless opinion.

## Just Add Water

Once the seeds of our analytical rubrics (e.g., HipHopetypes) are firmly rooted within the fertile landscape of your consciousness, you may add data from your independent investigations to test and see your understanding grow before your very eyes!

To allow for proper exposition of the relationship between GENIUS and Hip Hop, this book is divided into ten chapters of no more than ten pages of content apiece. Chapter 1 provides a brief historical contextualization of the origins of Hip Hop; readers will better appreciate Hip Hop's current GENIUS by having a reference point rooted in Hip Hop's original elements. Chapter 2 then outlines the analytical rubric that serves as the anchor for this manuscript: the HipHopetypes. All Hip Hop tracks observe certain rules and protocols; we review the criteria by which Hip Hop tracks should be judged. Also in Chapter 2, the vital distinction between Rap Music and Hip Hop is made before the contours of true Hip Hop music is fleshed out in Chapters 3 through 8, each one dedicated to one of the six HipHopetypes.

Chapter Nine focuses on the blurred lines of appreciation versus appropriation of this genre by mainstream culture. Chapter Ten then summarizes key points from the previous chapters and offers specific takeaways for readers still desirous for more information on the topic.

Lastly, it is important to note that while the substantive content of this book is appropriate for academic purposes (in addition to being suitable for fans of all types), this book freely employs a "Hip Hop style of writing." In other words, while the thoughts and concepts contained herein are certainly complex, the phraseology is not riddled with dense academic jargon. Rather than preemptively apologize for this text not sounding "academic enough," if anything, the author is selectively employing the rules of artistic expression frequently and freely employed within Hip Hop to more effectively communicate ideas. Thus, do no be alarmed over the occasional use of "slang" or "unconventional sentence construction" for sometimes, the most formal tone does not always strike the right chord.

# CHECK THE METHOD

Now, it is time to map out the contours of this creative force, or GENIUS. Since GENIUS (like "being cool") is such an abstract concept, to best frame this discussion we provide an analytical rubric entitled the HipHopetypes. The HipHopetypes encompass six different organizing themes that consistently manifest in virtually every expression of authentic Hip Hop. By understanding the HipHopetypes, recognizing them and how they work, we as a collective audience can better appreciate and approach this GENIUS more consistently.

When discussing the HipHopetypes, we provide an example-based approach so that the uninitiated and the expert alike can observe and evaluate the strength of the organizing theme for themselves. In accordance with the technology at our disposal currently, we shall provide names of designated tracks and performing/recording artists in addition to "YouTube links" so that readers can become active listeners as well. We realize these web links may not be permanent, but provided the song content does not change materially over time, the corresponding analysis and time stamps will still largely apply.

Yet, to be clear — this is not an all-inclusive text that will **BREAK DOWN** every Hip Hop lyric or technique imaginable. Nor is this book an all-encompassing, exhaustive encyclopedia that includes every awesome example from every dope artist imaginable. Nor is this book conceived as an all out diss of your favorite rapper simply because they do not appear to resolutely honor the precepts of Hip Hop. Instead, this manuscript is interested in fleshing out the common threads of Hip Hop's creative **GENIUS** and providing an analytical rubric to guide the reader towards greater understanding.

Thus, to better understand the intellectual beauty of what Hip Hop has to offer, one feature contained at the end of every chapter is "Before You Bounce." Each "Before You Bounce" section contains additional questions or critical thinking exercises that can be shared with family, friends or colleagues to deepen collective understanding of how Hip Hop works — from a cognitive standpoint. The presumption is that there is no better way to test one's understanding for a particular technique except by independently investigating it for themselves.

Largely absent from this text is sustained engagement with long-standing questions within Hip Hop that currently have no definitive answer. Is Hip Hop mysogynistic? Is Hip Hop to blame for the resurgent popularity of the word n*gger? Does Hip Hop promote violence and materialism? The answers to these questions (provided they exist) will not be found within these pages although we support the quest of these queries. Again, we are on a mission![7] Regardless of what society thinks about Hip Hop, our aim is to understand the creative thinking behind Hip Hop, practically speaking. In concluding this Introduction, much has been written about **who** helped inspire Hip Hop, **what** Hip Hop is or what it represents, **when** Hip Hop began, **where** Hip Hop got its first (beat) break and the social/economical/political reasons as to **why** Hip Hop got started and has not finished yet. Now is the time to discuss the **how**, or **GENIUS** behind Hip Hop.

## BEFORE YOU BOUNCE

- **KNOW** the definition of **GENIUS**

- Some examples of **GENIUS**, as showcased within these pages, may be expressed through strong language

- All of our references employ the MLA (Modern Language Association) style and are located in our **APPENDIX A, NOTATION**

- Especially for the uninitiated, songs with which any and every true Hip Hop aficionado should be familiar are designated as CLASSIC

# 1

# CONTEXTUALIZATION

Background on the Underground Sound

# A SHORT RECAP OF A LONG HISTORY

As with most concepts, before expanding to more intricate and complex ideas, it behooves us to first start with the basic history of Hip Hop.

If you ever wondered where did Hip Hop come from, or what is its origin and meaning, then now is the time to quickly address these inquiries. Contrary to popular belief and rumor, Hip Hop did not come straight from the beaches of Malibu, California during Spring Break just last year. Generally, the roots of Hip Hop stretch back to Africa with the call and response techniques made common of several verbally based, griot cultures.[1] Specifically, modern Hip Hop came from low-income, urban areas in the late 1970s. At this point in our country's history, many were still unclear on the future direction of the nation. The United States of America, home of the great democratic experiment, is in many ways still a work in progress and thus did not always operate optimally when it came to its stated ideals of life, liberty and the pursuit of happiness.

Without going into a long and painful historical lesson here, suffice to be said that early Americans' enslavement of African Americans and subsequent treatment of Native Americans while settling the "New World" under principles of Manifest Destiny made for some possible contradictions to these heralded democratic principles from the country's inception.[2] In the two centuries that followed after the country's founding, tensions behind building a strong and prosperous nation often conflicted with how other racial groups, such as Latino Americans in the southwest and Asian Americans in the west, were perceived as fitting into the American Dream.

Conversely, not all white Americans had an easy time settling in America and establishing prosperous lifestyles. The mass immigration movement of the early twentieth century demonstrated that many Irish, Jewish and Italian American immigrants were denigrated and separated by neighborhoods within the large urban metropolises (i.e., ghettos) and had a difficult time integrating into the mainstream. However, over time, many whites or at least those who presented as white, encountered **LESS FRICTION** whilst pursuing the "American Dream."[3] Why? Well, there were concrete and systemic social, legal and economic barriers institutionalized from the country's beginning that frustrated one's "pursuit of happiness" especially if one was visibly identifiable or black.[4] Again, without belaboring our nation's long and rich history on race relations, after the Era of Enslavement ended, Jim Crow segregationist laws, voting rights restrictions, convict leasing programs, redlining housing practices and unchecked vigilantism were some of the barriers between blacks and the American Dream, most especially for those living in the south up until the mid-1950s.

Then World War II changed everything.

The nation's response to the war required large investments of human capital — of all races and genders. The demands of war required that society relax its more traditional discriminatory stance on interpersonal relations and accordingly, many blacks "and women"[5] migrated from the economically depressed south towards northern cities where they could more easily land industrial or government employment. After the war, many cities with more diversified demographics had to contend with restructuring social order. Racial tensions flared in many of these growing cities, crystallized by a nationwide Civil Rights Movement that sought to affirm promises made to all Americans in the country's founding documents: the Declaration of Independence and the United States Constitution.

The decades-old, groundbreaking Civil Rights Movement largely came to a head during the 1960s with the revolutionary non-violence movement that culminated in the passage of the 1964 Civil Rights Act and the 1965 Voting Rights Act. While the nation essentially pledged to change some of its historically problematic "racial habits" on paper by way of new laws on the books, in practice, old habits were still hard to completely break.

By the 1970s, those formerly maligned Irish, Jewish and Italian immigrants of the 1920s were now accepted as "white" in contrast to the large influx of black and brown individuals who now populated large metropolitan areas like New York City, all looking for a piece of the American Dream. Blacks now occupied the ghettos that Irish, Jewish and Italian immigrants once inhabited and fled for the safer suburbs.[6] And worse, with stagflation (unemployment + inflation) slowing down the American economy in the early 1970s coupled with the aftershocks of systematically racist practices from merely a decade ago, many blacks found themselves stuck in the ghettoes with no clear path up or out in successful pursuit of the Horatio Alger myth and the American Dream.[7] The future looked bleak for many indeed.

Except for the pioneers of Hip Hop.

It is out of these bleak, maligned, economically depressed and resource-deprived ghettos of the mostly black and Latino South Bronx (as in, New York City) from whence the first vibrations of Hip Hop were first felt in the late 1970s. Now, it has grown into an international, billion-dollar phenomena where white listeners are the dominant consumers in America.[8] Currently, many within mainstream society freely patronize Hip Hop not necessarily for political, but personal reasons that differ markedly from the originator's reasons for engaging the craft.[9] This recent development is ironic when considering that Hip

Hop's originators were driven by social forces that largely prevented and frustrated their ability to participate within the mainstream. What accounted for this original exclusion? Was it just random? Or was it something else...like racism?

# THREE THE HARD WAY

Racism is irrational and illogical. Fine. Now that we have pushed this kernel of truth out of the way, the fact remains that many rational people must devise rational responses to racism, ergo this manuscript. From the country's inception, many early White Americans have had an obsession or preoccupation with race ever since "moving" Native Americans out of the way in the name of Manifest Destiny and utilizing the "necessary evil" of enslavement as the most efficient means of developing this "New World."[10]

While not all whites owned slaves, much of America was still a slave society (just like all members of society presently do not own cars, but much of our society and daily life is significantly affected by their presence, functionality and use within society).[11] Further, what we now know to be morally reprehensible today was both legal and commonplace during the Era of Enslavement. Yet, this slave society could not have existed for more than two centuries unless many respected members of society devised working rationales. Specifically, there are three irrefutable historical themes that operated together as an "intellectual shorthand" and provided white members of the slave sociey with just enough social momentum to combat the rational argument against slavery (as espoused in the original Declaration of Independence).[12] While these rationales would normally wilt under critical scrutiny individually, they worked together to maintain an efficient system. The three prongs of the "Unholy Trinity" are:

## Romantic Racialism

Romantic Racialism was a very influential 19th century theme that propagated the narrative that blacks were actually **SUPERIOR** to whites, but only within limited, subjugated contexts.[13] Thus, black slaves were lauded for their physical stature and skill, but only in relation to how their production directly benefitted the plantation owner. Blacks were seen as physically gifted and were also admired for their ability to sing, dance and "praise the Lord" despite their oppressed existence. A false sense of racial comity developed where many whites were convinced that they actually liked and appreciated blacks, but it was not a deep abiding love or respect. At an early stage, blacks were primarily valued and appropriated for their ability to "perform" only.

## Femininity

Femininity focused on the enslaved black's relationship with his white captor. The heighth of fantasy was for whites to go to bed guilt-free at night, knowing that the enslaved blacks who worked at their plantations did so because they somehow wanted to or enjoyed it. This fictive narrative stems from the general anthromorpification of races to genders, wherein the white race was seen as "masculine" due to its ability to build and design society whereas members of the black race was seen as a "feminine" race, or more docile and better suited for servile positions — whether male or female.[14] Hence, this narrative lured many a white plantation owner into believing that the enslaved present simply had no other lot in life but to protect and serve.

## Negrophobia

Negrophobia developed later in the Era of Enslavement and was a preemptive narrative used to justify and defend whites against threatening blacks. The only issue here is that such justifications often required great leaps of logic. Blacks were enslaved mostly by whites against their will. Many blacks resisted, rebelled or at least, thought about doing so. Many whites placed themselves in the proverbial shoes of the enslaved and thought about the anger and outrage they would feel if stripped of their humanity, dignity or respect. Many whites then feared the "backlash" they might receive from the enslaved if freedom for all was ever obtained. Thus, any perceived black anger, notwithstanding its logical basis, was to be immediately distrusted as dangerous and had to be quelled instantly — forcefully if need be.

Negrophobia later expanded to include the unexplained, fiery hate that many whites exhibited towards blacks. For instance, members of vigilante groups such as the Ku Klux Klan often cited fears of miscegenation, rape and joblessness for whites if blacks were allowed to run amok unchecked, thereby requiring the need to keep the "negro in his place."[15] This negrophobia fueled many of our country's lynchings[16] and other terrorist acts of violence against members of the black community and their allies. Notwithstanding the exceptional cases of Nat Turner and Denmark Vessey's separate uprisings that were successfully squashed, there is little historical evidence of mass black aggression that justified sustained attacks of whites upon blacks.

# DIVINE RESPONSE TO UNHOLY TRINITY

While principles of the Unholy Trinity may apply to any and all persons, this country has an established history of employing them consistently and explicitly against blacks. Thus, any well-informed citizen must interrogate the narrative that American Democracy and its "melting pot" in society were achieved without any morally dubious measures that contradicted American democratic principles.

The historical narratives of Romantic Racialism, Femininity and Negrophobia comprise and constitute the Unholy Trinity, which still influence race relations between blacks and whites today. Non-whites intuitively learns the contours of life as shaped by the Unholy Trinity, especially when the experience is made more acute through the lens of poverty. The three Unholy Trinity prongs work together as a destructive force since they collude to confuse the mainstream public about the true value of black humanity. Hip Hop artists may not necessarily consciously sit down and compose songs and other original ideas with the Unholy Trinity in mind *per se*, but they are consciously trying and vying for the dignity and respect that the Unholy Trinity institutionally and systematically denies.

Yet, if anything, we see that despite the trials and tribulations, the heartache and hypocrisy, black Americans have yet to systematically institutionalize an organized destructive force against another group of people within this country. Temporary "race riots" therefore do not qualify. Instead, by giving voice to their documented and validated frustrations through the gifts of style and song, we see that such creative energies cement black Americans' status as **QUINTESSENTIAL** Americans. Think of Hip Hop as forever being "in conversation" with the Unholy Trinity; and within the midst of this tension over humanity, dignity and respect is where Hip Hop lives...

# ABOUT THAT SOUND

Music, at its greatest can be described as a spiritual phenomena that can change the vibration of an individual's emotions and influence their feelings in a powerfully moving way. Or at the bare minimum, music can be distilled down to a literal vibration or combination of soundwaves. As most of us humans are made of flesh, these soundwaves can literally penetrate the skin and can be absorbed by the listener.[17] Now, we shall observe how these vibrations operate within a Hip Hop context. There are five essential parts to any Hip Hop track: **BEAT, VOCALS, HOOK, SAMPLE & MESSAGE.** Notice the symmetry with **THE ELEMENTS** of Hip Hop listed in the first row of the chart below (which will receive additional attention in Chapter 2):

| DJay | Emcee | B-boy/girl | Graffiti | Knowledge of Self |
|---|---|---|---|---|
| beat | vocals | hook | sample | message |
| without a beat, there is no rhythm and no song, mere speech results; beats are often created by DJs; beats have different temperatures ranging from **HOT** to **COOL** | vocals or lyrics are often created by MCs; range from **linear** (one thought sequentially follows the next) to **abstract** (appears more random in sequence & relation of ideas); from serious to humorous | the hook corresponds to B-boys & B-girls since the hook is often played during the break beat, or the "catchiest" part of the song that motivates people to dance & express selves through their bodies | samples CAN serve as the beat itself or can be included as additional "add-ons" to literally illustrate the musical artists' artistic flare - most Hip Hop samples help the MC paint the picture | most Hip Hop tracks are purposeful and have an intended message as a result - all messages do not have to be "deep," but do have to push the listener in a particular direction |

The beat is arguably the most important part of the song — not the vocals — since it is foundational and is likely the first aspect of the song that one will encounter. The beat also sets the tone of how to receive the message contained within the vocals (if any). The two major poles of beat temperatures are **HOT** and **COOL.**

With a **HOT** Beat, one can feel their pulse quicken as the rhythm is likely punctuated with strong, solid bass notes. The dominant beat literally helps one's heart "keep pace," as the quickening of one's pulse or heart rate means you have "extra" ability to move faster.[18] For **HOT** beats, the **GENIUS** behind heavier syncopation and more emphasis on "bass" is that bass literally "resonates" more so with the listener.[19] **HOT** beats are typically "faster" in contrast to **COOL** beats which generally are slower or have fewer beats per minute and thus are not quite as good for energizing and inspiring a crowd of strangers to assemble and gyrate on a dance floor. Hence, it is more common to hear tracks with **HOT** beats "in da club" or on commercial radio airwaves.

However, with a **COOL** beat, one can hear oneself "think" — there is less syncopation and less "distraction" for the listener so that more concentration can be dedicated to the vocals, verbal samples and resulting message. **COOL** beats frequently employ piano or string instrumentation and commonly utilize looping beat techniques so that the listener can literally "get into a groove" and not worry about a changing beat. The "security" in knowing that the beat remains steady allows for increased alertness for more clever puns, subtle messaging and slight intonations in voice that help to convey a larger message.

| Temperature of Hip Hop Beats ||
| Hot Beat | Cool Beat |
| --- | --- |
| • little thought required (of listener)<br>• high movement stimulated (of listener)<br>• appeal to emotion (of listener)<br>• heavy syncopation<br>• emphasis on hook<br>• song structure more formulaic | • much thought required (of listener)<br>• little movement stimulated (of listener)<br>• appeal to intellect (of listener)<br>• light syncopation<br>• emphasis on lyricism<br>• song structure more abstract |
| Ex: **"Show Me What U Got,"** Jay-Z | Ex: **"Tekzilla,"** Common & DJ Hi-Tek |

# BEFORE WE PROCEED

With the Unholy Trinity as part of our background, it is important for us to **KEEP IT REAL** and be explicit about another facet of Hip Hop as it relates to being either a conscious (or subconscious) response to the Unholy Trinity. Hip Hop is one of the few industries in the world that was created and still is **LARGELY** influenced (not necessarily controlled) by black males. It is a quasi-independent means of generating capital and with this autonomy comes independent thought and action. This self-sufficiency on multiple levels has liberating qualities in many respects. For to move one's body in new, free-flowing ways, to express one's sexuality, to voice pointed social critiques forcefully, while breaking grammar rules and using socially impolite profanity, to tap into one's own "unconscious" freestyle flow (as in speaking in different tongues), to create new sounds and new songs, to feel free to bring people together in a loving atmosphere — this perhaps is a remix on the common goals of life, liberty and the "pursuit of happyness."[20]

Yet, despite these potentially positive qualities, no less than three Congressional Hearings involving Hip Hop music have been held (1985, 1994 & 2007), the earliest form taking place in 1985 courtesy of advocacy by the Parents Music Resource Center (PMRC).[21] The PMRC's efforts at raising awareness were successful and resulted in an agreement with the Recording Industry Association of America (RIAA) where recording companies would voluntarily place warning labels on music with violent or sexually explicit lyrics. Hence, the PMRC is largely responsible for the "Parental Advisory" labels we routinely see on Rap Music albums today. While the initial target of PMRC was the "Filthy Fifteen," or mostly rock music songs, Rap Music was soon to take center stage in the 1990s when Luke Campbell's 2 Live Crew was found "obscene" by a Florida judge.[22] This court ruling set in motion a maelstrom whereby Rap Music would now forever be placed under national scrutiny. As an example of such continued scrutiny, in a 2005 *New York Times* editorial, the author stated that Rap Music:

> started out with a broad palette of themes but has increasingly evolved into a medium for worshipping misogyny, materialism and murder.[23]

This editorial's cogent criticism succinctly encapsulates the **"frequently asserted knocks (or criticisms) expressed in mainstream culture"** against Hip Hop. Given the length of that last sentence, we conveniently created a shorthand for future reference within the text: **F.A.K.E. M.C.s**.

**NOTE**: We substitute "mayhem" for the word "murder" from the *New York Times* editorial since mayhem is a broader term that encompasses violence (including murder), anti-authority, rejection of middle class mores, glamorization of drug use among others.

| The 3 F.A.K.E. M.C.s vs. Hip Hop | | |
|:---:|:---:|:---:|
| Misogyny | Materialism | Mayhem |

The assertion that Hip Hop primarily supports Misogyny, Materialism and Mayhem is a serious allegation indeed. We must listen closely to see whether this is true.

# BEFORE YOU BOUNCE

- **KNOW** the (American) history behind Hop Hop's creation

- Commit to memory the **UNHOLY TRINITY**

- **YOUR TURN**: listen to several different Hip Hop tracks on your own — can you classify the beats as **COOL** or **HOT**?

- What do you think about the frequently asserted knocks expressed in mainstream culture against Hip Hop (i.e., **F.A.K.E. M.C.s**.)? Are they valid or invalid? Why or why not?

# 2

# DEFINITION

The Elementary Difference between
Rap Music & Hip Hop

# HIP HOP GETS A BAD RAP

Hip Hop is not monolithic; while many a club or festive party environment plays hardcore beats with people dancing and shaking all body parts interior and exterior, Hip Hop can be deeply philosophical, inspirational and educational. This range can appear confusing and contradictory to many. So now is the time to parse out the nuances since all Rap Music is not Hip Hop even though all Hip Hop is a part of a larger Rap Music culture. But to be clear, Rap Music **IS NOT** Hip Hop. Hip Hop by design contains messaging on or around socio/political/economical themes for both entertainment and education (i.e., "edutainment") whereas Rap Music is the commodification and commercialization of rap culture associated with such messaging for entertainment primarily.

| Difference in Qualities between Rap Music & Hip Hop | |
| --- | --- |
| **Rap Music** | **Hip Hop** |
| • commercialized & commodified Hip Hop<br>• made for entertainment primarily<br>• little connection to the Hip Hop elements and/or HipHopetypes<br>• mainstream exposure (e.g., radio airplay, videos)<br>• more formulaic in design | • validated & venerated Rap Music<br>• made for expression & enrichment primarily<br>• heavy reliance on/recognition of Hip Hop elements and/or HipHopetypes<br>• largely "underground" (e.g., word of mouth)<br>• more abstract in execution |

Hip Hop is so strong, that indigenous Hip Hop artists as far away as New Zealand and Australia emulate the patterns of expression exhibited by urban youth who properly channel Hip Hop as a constructive outlet.[1] Such indigenous artists face similar struggles for survival and respect as statistical minorities within their own countries as with many American artists responsible for fostering

Hip Hop's powerful outlet of expression (the majority of whom are disaffected African American and Latino urban youth). As it stands, American mainstream media is seen and enjoyed by diverse audiences not just in America, but all over the world. Thus, it is imperative that further inquiry is conducted about which Hip Hop artists infiltrate the public consciousness and how.

For instance, female rapper Iggy Azalea recently burst onto the mainstream Hip Hop scene in 2014 as part of one of the fastest growing genres within one of the world's largest and most influential media industries generating upwards of $10 billion annually.[2] For many youth of color internationally, Hip Hop, its music and associated culture collectively represent a shared social experience of significant value outside of pop culture's dictates. Yet, Iggy Azalea represents a different look and sound from Hip Hop music that is truly underground whether in America or in the land "down under."

Hip Hop has now evolved into an important tool used both to inform and influence economic, social and political identity for people of color on a global scale. Using profiles of select artists and with analytical deconstruction of several choice musical selections, we will illustrate how Hip Hop practitioners worldwide are agents of social change and transformation while critiquing hegemony in the worldwide struggle for dignity and respect. This rich source of history and culture can no longer be ignored by academia and others.

When combined together, we see that Hip Hop, its music and principles, raises self-esteem, communal awareness and global responsibility. Thus, we must be clear, or **STRAIGHT UP** about what Hip Hop represents and the time-honored components that comprise its composition. These essential ingredients are known colloquially within Hip Hop circles as **THE ELEMENTS.**[3]

# THE ELEMENTS

Hip Hop means so many things to so many different people. This is all well and good. But as with anything human, Hip Hop has a structure. Just as one learns the alphabet before learning to read, one must know **THE ELEMENTS** before learning to listen to Hip Hop. It only makes sense to understand this basic structure before exploring how Hip Hop artists manipulate and harness the basic elements for their expressive creations.

Hip Hop is largely credited as being founded by pioneers from New York City. In many ways it is unfair to limit Hip Hop's creation to a small list of individuals for it truly was a collective creation. However, a couple names most commonly associated with initially making Hip Hop known within the mainstream are DJ Kool Herc and Afrika Bambaataa.[4] These pioneers started an organic model of development comprising five basic elements that every disciple should know. What follows is not an exhaustive review but merely a brief overview of Hip Hop in its most basic form since any serious discussion of Hip Hop must discuss the correct elements in the correct manner.

The five elements of Hip Hop are as follows:

- DJing                                        - Emceeing
                - Knowledge of Self
- B-Boying/Girling                             - Graffiti

Hip Hop is more than mere Rap Music; it is an ever-evolving way of life, culture and expression. It is complex, yet accessible. Its chief components may be organized into five different categories often not readily apparent in Rap Music videos and Top 40 playlists:

# 1. DJing

First is the Deejay, or DJ for short. Originally, the letters "D" and "J" stood for "Disc Jockey," or the individual in charge of making the appropriate musical selections for radio airplay or more locally for the enjoyment of partygoers in attendance. This person "keeps the beat" by playing the right songs that the crowd will love. But DJs have evolved into so much more. Now, the letters "DJ" are akin to a professional title such as "Sargeant" or "Officer" when used among those in Hip Hop circles by those who appreciate the DJ's skill. For above all, of all the elements within the Hip Hop multi-verse, deejaying is arguably the most difficult. The DJ obtains respect because he or she is responsible for directing the energy of a large throng of individuals, many of whom never met before. Then, by careful planning and observation, the deejay must put together a formula that entails a proper assemblage of vibrations and sounds that will get the crowd "hype" or stimulated to generate a higher energy output. Without the deejay, there is no "party." What you have instead is a mere "gathering."

DJs also produce and create beats for performing artists or Emcees. This too, is not as easy as it sounds (literally). Books have been written about how DJs effectively sample older songs to create newer ones, so we will not belabor the reader with such details here.[4] Suffice to say, picking the best part of a song and looping it repeatedly is an underrated skill that showcases originality at its finest. Many new Hip Hop tracks were created from well-known songs that no one else thought to sample from. Other samples are found from the tireless quest of searching for that overlooked flare of musical **GENIUS** otherwise buried in the middle of a pedestrian album or obscure song. This process, entitled **DIGGING IN THE CRATES** symbolizes a larger work ethic and dedication to the craft of Hip Hop.[5]

## 2. B-boying/girling

Next, B-boying and B-girling are the official names we give to those who exclusively perform and perfect Hip Hop dance moves to Hip Hop beats. The full name is "breakdancer" and can be also known as "breaking" but this element title has since been truncated to "B-Boy." Break dance moves are unique as they are punctuated by crisp, defined, robotic movements (known as popping or locking) and demonstrate creativity and mastery of body control with respect to fine motor movement. Break dancing can also range to the entirely expressive and acrobatic whereby the whole body is involved in generating sufficient energy to spin repeatedly on one's head, or rotating around in a circular motion on one's shoulders with the legs flared out in the air (otherwise known as the "helicopter"). In both instances, creativity is the currency as entire groups of teams or "crews" will do battle, or compete with one another, freezing key poses and even flipping or performing tricks off the bodies of one another.

This non-violent way of competing for respect or "props" was a constructive alternative to real turf battles in the neighborhood that usually ended in bodily harm for someone. Now, break dancing championships are held internationally and Hip Hop as a dance genre is now mainstream.[6] As we all know, from the local YMCA to international cruise ships, Hip Hop dance classes are an extremely popular as well as beneficial source of exercise. Those who can move rhythmically to Hip Hop sounds are indeed mesmerizing to watch.

## 3. Emceeing

Thirdly, once music is on the scene and bodies have gathered to move to the music, early in Hip Hop's evolution, the MC or Master of

Ceremonies was involved to help direct the crowd and keep the high energy exchange flowing and growing. Often times, the MC was in fact the deejay, as simple commands such as "Somebody! Anybody! Everybody...SCREAM!" would help keep the crowd engaged via the age-old black cultural tradition of "call and response." When people think of Hip Hop today, they may mostly think only of the MC and focus on one particular individual on stage. However, in its original conception, the crowd of participants was central and the deejay was the most important person in the room.

The MC's role has since expanded over the years to be the focal point or figurehead of many Hip Hop circles as MCs over the years evolved from delivering party commands to rapping rhythmically over beats the deejays assembled. To increase the amount of substantive content that would be shared over a microphone, deejays grew more creative in sampling or putting together new songs created from older ones.

In other words, observant deejays noticed that the crowd became excited and wanted to dance the hardest during the BRIDGE, or best part of the song when there was less vocals and more instrumentation during the "grooviest" part of a track. This part of the song was also known as the "break beat." Clever deejays, looking to make this moment last forever and extend the good feeling created by dancers present, began to use two turn tables connected to play the same song on two different records so that once the break beat ended on one record, they would be able to keep the beat by extending the sound on the second record. This pre-selected song part is called a "sample."

This "looping" technique of sampled tracks now common to many Hip Hop songs was absolutely innovative given the technological innovations at the time. Back when record players were the heighth of technology, hitting a simple "rewind" button was out of the question.

Even still, silence results when pressing the rewind button and the whole trick was to maintain a smooth, fluid and uninterrupted sound.

Speaking of fluidity, MCing represents the talented vocalist who has mastered the art of "the rhyme." Rather than subject the audience to a vulgar and base display of unimaginative lyrics, Hip Hop has nurtured and cultured dedicated lyricists who regale the crowd with clever wordplay, creative constructs and marvelous metaphors — all while rhyming! Lyrical skill speaks for itself (get it?) and is nothing less than a confident declaration of intelligence. As our aim is to establish a cogent rubric of understanding Hip Hop's overall GENIUS, we are not afforded the opportunity to analyze every written line as other websites and hopefully future writings will continue to do so. But be of good cheer, there is still so much to explore!

## 4. Graffiti

Fourth is the element that refers to the artistic, symbolic representation of Hip Hop culture outside of most dancehalls and house parties. "Graf" is short for graffiti. While we do not condone the damage or destruction of public buildings, many scholars have recognized much of the renderings produced by graffiti artists as powerful artistic expressions of color, shapes and ideas.[7]

Another way to look at the picture is to ask "When does the public participate in public art?" From the shape of our buildings to the color of our walls, public art is often privately negotiated by a very small group of people. Graffiti's initial foray as part of the Hip Hop Movement was an interruption of a narrative that largely rendered black and brown people within inner cities invisible. Broad, bubbly, colorful strokes on public buildings in very public places interrupts that narrative and reminds the viewer of the existence of another.[8] Whether you agree or disagree, the graffiti artist is at the very minimum successful in attracting your attention and alerting you to their presence. Whether it be an act of political protest or vandalism is for you to decide — but what is the difference between local graffiti artists or corporate marketers such as McDonald's & Bud Light plastering their name all around town? One pays while the other sprays?

## 5. Knowledge of Self

Lastly and fifthly is "Knowledge of Self," which is the element that refers to Hip Hop's long-standing historical connection with substantive issues of social justice. Many believe that the rap videos they see on television which appear to glorify material acquisition and misogyny are representative of Hip Hop. They are mistaken. Hip Hop comes from a tradition of marginalized black and brown poets from the inner city environs of New York and has maintained its tradition of speaking out for those who are disaffected by shortcomings in our larger social systems. Hip Hop has not only provided a voice for such insightful expression, but has also offered inspiration for those wishing to improve their local communities.

Knowledge of Self is arguably the most difficult of the five elements to grasp since it is more abstract. Knowledge of Self is an attempt to "build" up oneself and those within one's cypher, or close circle (not necessarily closed circle) with the belief that the "truth shall set you free." We should be clear, while the pursuit of knowledge in and of itself is always a good thing, in this case, the question is why? Why would Hip Hop disciples arbitrarily pursue Knowledge of Self as opposed to Knowledge of Art or Knowledge of Family Tree? Whereas the end point of such a journey is open-ended and is often symbolized or referenced by the opening of the "third eye,"[9] the genesis of this quest is largely presumed and thus unspoken. Here, we submit that all quests of Knowledge of Self are in response to the Unholy Trinity, which are three irrefutable historical narratives that conspired (and still conspire) to deflate, denigrate and demean black self-esteem.

# OUR HIPHOPOSOPHY

Now that we understand that the Knowledge of Self element was constructed in response to the Unholy Trinity, we see that the fifth element has contours that must be fleshed out further. Hip Hop disciples practice or observe Knowledge of Self by employing at least one or more of the **HIPHOPETYPES** — an artistic theme with a purpose rooted in honoring the culture of Hip Hop.

HipHopetypes are general patterns of thought that appear loose, random and uncoordinated on the surface, but upon closer inspection, provide proof of a **HIPHOPOLOGY**, or a complex mapping of an incredibly consistent ethos of principles and protocols that comprise Hip Hop culture. The six HipHopetypes are as follows:

| Rejection | Prescription | Aspiration | Description | Demonstration | Recognition |
|---|---|---|---|---|---|
| Unholy Trinity Antidote to the corresponding Anti-Creative Forces | | | | | |
| exclusion | indecision | desolation | delusion | marginalization | invalidation |

In looking at the difference between Rap Music and Hip Hop, one must ask "How **OFTEN** and how **OBVIOUS** is reverence & reference made to **THE ELEMENTS** and **HIPHOPETYPES**?" Purely Rap Music tracks are typically devoid of such references whereas Hip Hop tracks are typically defined by such references. In concert, the HipHopetypes are locked "in conversation" with the Unholy Trinity and are actively fighting against structural, institutional, systemic forces on a grand scale that have historically frustrated the efforts of many to enjoy life.

Only because they were black.

Or fill in the blank. By nature we are social creatures and wish to be included, respected and loved. Hip Hop as an antidote to the Unholy Trinity neutralizes the destructive nature of others by facilitating the creative forces of those of like mind.

Or should we say, of "sound" mind and body?

# WE'RE GOING IN

The six subsequent chapters profile the HipHopetypes with at least ten examples apiece to illustrate how each concept works. These examples are not all-encompassing, representative or definitive — they are just a brief foundational list of excellent examples to which you will undoubtedly add more as you BUILD upon your understanding. To show how ubiquitious the HipHopetypes are, each example session will start with the well-known track, "Juicy" by The Notorious B.I.G. (hereinafter referred to by his affectionate stage name, "Biggie Smalls"). Since this song is so iconic, it serves as an excellent reference point as many readers can see the familiar in new ways through the HipHopetypes. "Juicy" is quite versatile since it embodies all six HipHopetypes, further underscoring how they are not mutually exclusive while simultaneously illustrating how a track can exhibit characteristics of more than one HipHopetype.

Good news, bad news! Let's start with the bad news first. The bad news is that with all of the examples provided throughout the subsequent pages, not all tracks are likely to be songs with which you are familiar. Many are "older" songs or strictly underground songs that have never seen the light of day on mainstream radio. And uh, that might be precisely the point! However, the good news is that the HipHopetypes are broad and inclusive categories. Thus, you can apply the criteria right now to songs you hear today to determine whether or not a track is truly Hip Hop or not.

## Before You Bounce

- **KNOW THE ELEMENTS**

- **KNOW** the elementary differences between Rap Music and Hip Hop

- **YOUR TURN**: there is much debate on this topic, but based upon what you now know of **THE ELEMENTS** of Hip Hop, do you classify Iggy Azalea as Hip Hop or something else? How does she honor or evidence homage and respect of **THE ELEMENTS**, if she is to be qualified and classified as Hip Hop in the first place?

# 3

# <u>REJECTION</u>

HipHopetype #1

| Rejection | Description | Demonstration | Prescription | Aspiration | Recognition |
|---|---|---|---|---|---|
| **HipHopetypes Corresponding with Honored Hip Hop Elements** | | | | | |
| MC | DJ | Graffiti | Knowledge of Self | B-boy/girl | ALL |
| **Unholy Trinity Antidote to the Corresponding Anti-Creative Forces** | | | | | |
| **FEAR** | | | **FASCINATION** | | |
| exclusion | delusion | marginalization | indecision | desolation | invalidation |
| **HipHopetypes Ethos as Evidence of Creative GENIUS** | | | | | |
| **FAITH** | | | **FACILITATION** | | |
| inclusion | clarity | empowerment | wisdom | optimism | dignity & respect |

# THE HITS KEEP COMING

Who wants to feel dissed?

By most accounts, no one.

We as human beings are innately social creatures. Sure, there are those among us who avoid crowds or eschew large gatherings. But on the whole, many of us would agree with the age-old adage that "no person is an island." And certainly, most of us would agree that being alone as a result of being dissed, or disrespected or made to feel less than great is not a good feeling.

Thus, in returning to our original question, the vast majority of us — even the most "hardcore" among us — may not say it, but they believe that it is vitally important to feel part of a larger group. In other words, while many want to be left alone from time to time, no one truly wants to feel left out *all the time*. Hence, associating with a larger group, one that recognizes your special worth, value and individuality is not only healthy, but is necessary.[1] Many of us receive this affirmation daily through our immediate families, circle of friends, school classmates, religious affiliations, social clubs, professional associations, sports teams, etc. In all of these examples and in others unnamed, people build their personal identity partly through the identification with a larger group with whom the individual communes. In every case, there must exist a connection — otherwise, there is no investment and as a result, no empathy offered, nor none received.

We say all this to say that if people innately draw strength from feeling generally included, then does it not logically follow that the opposite would happen if the opposite happened? In other words, would people not feel deflated if they felt rejected? In other words, who would want to feel dissed?

While most do not want to be dissed or rejected, we all have been on the short end of the social stick at some point in time. The nature of the human experience makes it virtually impossible for any one to grow, mature and live a full adult life without being treated rudely or rejected — whether correctly or incorrectly — at some point in time.

Within the context of Hip Hop, as originated through the lens of historically marginalized urban black and brown youth, rejection takes on an entirely different meaning. Within the context of black history in America, rejection first meant only being measured as 3/5 of a person and not being worthy enough to be classified as a full citizen and vote.[2] Early treatment of blacks during the Era of Enslavement defined rejection in every respect. To acknowledge black blood flowing through one's veins was to acknowledge that politically, economically and socially that one's life would be forever different — and not for the better — albeit at no fault of their own.[3]

As briefly touched upon in the brief historical recap in Chapter One, structural and systemic denial of rights, services and opportunities resulted in many black Americans being and feeling rejected. Many Hip Hop artists have been born into this historically problematic legacy and also face similar circumstances of rejection as did the generations before them. For instance, today's current Hip Hop generation does not face issues in employment caused about by rejection from segregationist policies enforced by state law, *per se*.[4] But instead, studies demonstrate that it is harder for a person with a "black-sounding" name to land a job,[5] or that it is easier for a white convict to obtain a call back for an interview compared to a black applicant with no criminal record.[6] These data points (not anecdotes) evidence continued maintenance of the Unholy Trinity that may also be framed as rejection at the very least. During the segregationist era, individuals were more transparent about the racist rationales used to justify segregation. Now, the data merely confirms what many may have believed or "felt" to be true – that opportunities for success are often more limited for a non-white person despite public adherence to rules of "fair play" and "equal opportunity" for all. Horatio Alger would be pressed indeed to find a logical or rational reason for such consistent rejection other than considering racism *as a factor*.

In order to cope with this deep, pervading, overarching sense of rejection, many Hip Hop artists have responded in a number of creative ways to these distressing social conditions to make themselves and their listeners feel better. Think of Hip Hop as openly engaging these tropes, not too unlike the early tradition of "Blues" music.[7]

Rejection within Hip Hop can take a variety of different forms and can range from the direct and deeply personal (e.g., having heart broken on a date) to the indirect and abstract (e.g., critiques upon society & law). Thus, the existing narratives and life experiences the listener brings with them to the track-listening experience affects to what degree these stories of rejection resonate. Many whites in the suburbs may interpret these feelings of angst as "in tune" with their struggles for identity when coming of age within their own suburban households.[8] Meanwhile, others may hear larger, broader themes of all-encompassing oppression against which they feel they *still* struggle.

Regardless, it is time to proceed. If you are a true "Hip Hop Head," then you already have these tracks in your possession (smile). If not, for whatever reason, you likely can find such tracks online from a variety of different sources. Feel free to purchase these tracks to support the artist and to support the survival of real Hip Hop.

# YOU'RE WELCOME

In the ten examples that follow, consider the Unholy Trinity and how it may inform or influence the track profiled. Representative examples of the Rejection HipHopetype include, but are not limited to:

| CLASSIC Rejection Example #1 | | | |
|---|---|---|---|
| Artist | Track | Sample | When |
| Biggie Smalls | "Juicy" (1994) | "This album is dedicated... to all the teachers that told me I'd never amount to nuthin..." | 0:06 mark (during introduction of the track) |
| LINK: https://www.youtube.com/watch?v=4M0ObL56C0A | | | |

**Brief Analysis:** In all actuality and all jokes aside, it is both disheartening and disappointing for a teacher to be a discouraging presence to our youth given their job description to presumably do just the opposite. Biggie's line speaks to how the Unholy Trinity affects even the youth trapped in the ghetto and more importantly, that he as a youth realizes this to be so.

Biggie either wittingly or unwittingly spoke to the phenomena of low teacher expecations that negatively impact student performance.[9] Given the disproportionality of higher suspension and expulsion rates for black males — especially in light of the disproportionate amount of elementary educators that "just happen" to be white female,[10] Biggie in a mere couple of lines exhorts the listener to reconsider whether our educational system is working as it should for all American children, regardless of their race. Additional studies make the problematic connection between early exits from school and early entries into the prison industrial complex.[11] Hence, Biggie suggests that while he may not have had the specific academic language and theory to say so, that he clearly understood how his life was impacted by — and worse, rejected by — the Unholy Trinity at such a young and tender stage in life.

| Rejection Example #2 | | | |
|---|---|---|---|
| **Artist** | **Track** | **Sample** | **When** |
| Jay-Z | "Win or Lose" [remix] (@ 2011)<br><br>by Mobb Deep feat. Nas & Jay-Z | "All the teachers couldn't reach me and my momma couldn't beat me hard enough to mask the pain of my pop not seeing me — so! With that stain on my membrane, got on my pimp game, 'F**k the world!' — my defense came." | 3:10 mark |
| **LINK:** https://www.youtube.com/watch?v=Ud_OdFxzibk | | | |
| **BONUS LINK:** https://www.youtube.com/watch?v=gMo9IsqPRwU&spfreload=1 | | | |

**Brief Analysis:** Jay-Z intimates that his life situation, as impliedly impacted by the Unholy Trinity, was not ideal as a child to say the least. Jay-Z at the time perhaps did not fully grasp why his life was challenged, but with a fractured family life, disengagement from school came next followed by his attempt to protect himself from further pain by literally labeling his rejection of the world as a defense to its rejection of him! Jay Z told himself "F**k the world," but perhaps this mindstate could be changed if he were allowed to fairly participate. It is unlikely Jay Z adopts this mantra *now* seeing how he depends upon generous patronage from "the world" to finance his family's publicly famous, luxurious lifestyle. Yet, we can imagine how damaging this mantra could be if a critical mass of disaffected black and brown young men still believe that this coping mechanism of walling off from the world is the only way to survive it.

**Bonus Analysis:** Similarly, at the 2:38 mark of the song "Channel 10" by the New York duo Capone N Noreaga, Noreaga seemingly out of nowhere exclaims "F*ck the world! The way the world cold dissed me...." These ten words intimate that his total life situation, as impliedly impacted by the Unholy Trinity, was making him feel "dissed." In response, he chooses to disengage from the world, and isolate himself from further rejection by mounting a callous defense to the ways of the world instead. This sense of social disaffection by marginalized urban youth was vividly captured by author Richard Wright when he teased out conditions that precipitated the creation of Bigger Thomas in the gripping novel "Native Son."[12]

| Rejection Example #3 | | | |
|---|---|---|---|
| **Artist** | **Track** | **Sample** | **When** |
| Phonte | "Not Enough" (2005)<br><br>by Little Brother | "DJs dissing the album before they check it; dealing with their managers and program directors..." | 0:32 mark |
| **LINK:** https://www.youtube.com/watch?v=TSV6RlStK1o | | | |

**Brief Analysis:** The North Carolina trio of Phonte, Rapper Big Pooh and DJ 9th Wonder (y'all!) appear to be venting some frustration in this track. Being a Hip Hop act from the south, not only do they face difficulty finding success as an underground act generally, but they also face a presumptive bias that assumes anyone not hailing from New York City (or Philadelphia) is automatically devoid of true skill. Phonte informs in the next line "...and even though I try not to stress it, sometimes it feels like a waste of time and not worth the effort." Here, their effort is appreciated since it reminds the listener that rejection is part of success.

| Rejection Example #4 | | | |
|---|---|---|---|
| **Artist** | **Track** | **Sample** | **When** |
| Cool C | "Life in the Ghetto" (1990) | "Dissed! But that's OK, that stuff happens everyday. To redeem yourself, forget that chick, find someone else." | 1:35 mark |
| **LINK:** https://www.youtube.com/watch?v=SptdxBKb5g8 | | | |

**Brief Analysis:** Here, the Philadelphian author is transparent about being dissed or rejected by a potential love interest. Rather than sulk or mope about the circumstance, or worse, internalize the rejection as evidence of a personal failing, Cool C provides both himself and the listener with a philosophical context that may help to deal with rejection when couched in the terms of the following line: "But that's the way that it goes when you're living in the ghetto."

## Rejection Example #5

| Artist | Track | Sample | When |
|---|---|---|---|
| Consequence | "Job Song" (2008) | "Now I'm in a situation that I can't pacify. So I'm looking through the paper skimming through the classifieds..." | 1:23 mark |
| LINK: https://www.youtube.com/watch?v=j_o3dJlGu6U | | | |

**Brief Analysis:** Here, Consequence cannot find a job. Worse, as he struggles against the implied forces of the Unholy Trinity, he is in a situation he "can't pacify," or rather cannot make out why his application keeps getting rejected. Perhaps he should change his last name.[13]

## *CLASSIC* Rejection Example #6

| Artist | Track | Sample | When |
|---|---|---|---|
| Slick Rick | "Mona Lisa " (1988) | "Great Scott! Are you a thief? Seems like you have a mouth full of gold teeth. Ha ha ha, I had to find that funny so I said: 'No Child, I work hard for the money.'" | 1:17 mark |
| LINK: https://www.youtube.com/watch?v=greKNLhdlNw | | | |

**Brief Analysis:** Slick Rick is none too amused over the fact that a potential love interest would think to insult him upon an initial chance encounter. Worse, earlier in the track, Slick Rick details how he went out of his way to show the young lady of interest charity and charm by offering to buy Ms. Mona Lisa a slice of pizza. While Ms. Lisa was blinded by Mr. Rick's smile, he did not see her rejection of him coming. Thus, the rest of the song is about Slick Rick's annoyed reaction over the young lady's assumption that he was perhaps criminally minded. Cold pizza indeed.

## Rejection Example #7

| Artist | Track | Sample | When |
|---|---|---|---|
| Cormega | "Love In, Love Out" (2002) | "My love is real, some earn it and some are unworthy. Some walk in the presence of men with thoughts to hurt me and wonder why I throw shade or stayed in myself — 'cause I'm me, plus I'm not betraying myself." | 1:34 mark |
| LINK: https://www.youtube.com/watch?v=yJqya0oWjew | | | |

**Brief Analysis:** Cormega shares the personal story of anguish after being rejected and hurt by his former colleague and friend, Nas. The pain and anguish of rejection is pretty clear when he inserts in the hook "Trust is a luxury I can't afford. Betrayal is something that I can't ignore." The point of the track is "underscored" via the **COOL** beat sampled by Isaac Hayes.[14]

## Rejection Example #8

| Artist | Track | Sample | When |
|---|---|---|---|
| 50 Cent | "Many Men" (2003) | "Many men, wish death upon me; blood in my eyes and I can't see." | 0:36 mark |
| LINK: https://www.youtube.com/watch?v=Ttk3IUKfn4U | | | |

**Brief Analysis:** 50 Cent states a valid case for feeling rejected by another in view of the fact that he was shot nine times by rivals — both in this song and in real life.[15] The chorus of this song illustrates the resulting guardedness that 50 Cent feels towards people he cannot trust, since his literal survival depends upon more supportive relationships in his life. After all, social rejection by one of another taken to its extreme can end in severe bodily harm or death. 50 Cent did not take kindly to his Rejection in this instance and his subsequent success was part of his revenge.

## Rejection Example #9

| Artist | Track | Sample | When |
| --- | --- | --- | --- |
| Nas | "Ether" (2001) | "Y'all just piss on me, sh*t on me, spit on my grave; talk about me, laugh behind my back but in my face; y'all some well wishers, friendly acting, envy hiding snakes; with your hands out for my money, man how much can I take?" | 1:21 mark |
| **LINK:** https://www.youtube.com/watch?v=0ePQKD9iBfU | | | |

**Brief Analysis:** Mr. Nasir bin Olu Dara Jones unleashes his wrath and fury upon Jay Z as the latter made the apparent mistake of publicly insulting, dissing or rejecting Nas. It appears from the sample lyric above that Nas is sore displeased that someone chose to diss, or reject him, for whatever the reason. The entire song is focused and stays "on message"; after listening, one would be wise not to commit the error of having Nas become cross with them unless they risk Rejection for themselves.

While Hip Hop fans celebrate and salivate over "diss tracks," it is important not to overlook why the diss track was made in the first place. Such tracks largely stem from the need to counter an initial attempt to publicly humiliate or embarrass an individual and can be seen as a self-preservation mechanism of one's positive self-image.

Other notable public "diss" exchanges involve the following Hip Hoppers:

| | |
| --- | --- |
| Kool Moe Dee vs. LL Cool J | Biggie Smalls/Junior Mafia vs. 2Pac/Outlawz |
| JJ Fadd vs. Sugar & Spice | 50 Cent vs. Rick Ross |
| Common vs. Ice Cube | Drake vs. Meek Mill |

For the record, after Nas "cleared the air" with the "Ether" track, Jay Z and Nas since reconciled and collaborated together (e.g., "Black Republican").

| Rejection Example #10 | | | |
|---|---|---|---|
| **Artist** | **Track** | **Sample** | **When** |
| Masta Ace | "Da Grind" (2004) | "And after it all, I still gotta perform, at three o'clock in the morn, after half the fans have gone — but it's fine." | 1:01 mark |
| **LINK:** https://www.youtube.com/watch?v=VtfCnslEUEo | | | |

**Brief Analysis:** Masta Ace brilliantly and poetically describes a scene not often depicted in glamorous rap music videos wherein thousands of screaming fans are depicted mouthing every word of the artists. Instead, Masta Ace offers a more humbling experience whereupon instead of being the leading act that comes on stage to perform around the respectable hour of 8:00 or 9:00pm, he finally has the opportunity to practice his craft when hardly anyone is around. The timing of his performance "at three o'clock in the morn," and the amount of people who stay to witness the performance "after half the fans are gone" are related to the amount of "respect" that he is receiving or not receiving rather. The lack of public support or positive feedback is not because Masta Ace is slacking or withholding effort. Mr. Ace informs us that when he is "putting my grind down, doing shows out of town" that he juggles the following job responsibilities:

| | |
|---|---|
| manager | tour planner |
| road manager | VP of marketing and promotions |
| call handler | producer |
| booking agent | arranger |
| choreagrapher | ["what a range of emotions!"] |

In other words, he is making himself transparent and is illustrating how part of staying true to his craft necessarily involves those evenings (or early mornings, rather) where he still has to decide to stay dedicated to the proposition even though everything is not going his way. Finally, as further evidence of his dogged determination to fight the feelings and failings of rejection, observe the sample featuring the rapper Nas around the 2:55 mark towards the song's conclusion.[16]

# Before You Bounce

- The **Rejection HipHopetype** speaks to the general angst one feels in being marginalized by the Unholy Trinity, or can be specific to one individual "getting dissed" by another individual or larger institution

- **FOCUS** not upon the Rejection, but upon the response to it — most narrators who choose to be transparent enough to share such information have usually figured out how to cope since — think of the video and concluding verse from the song "Many Men" by 50 Cent (Rejection Example #8)

- **YOUR TURN**: Can you write a song about a situation in which you were dissed? Would it be a humorous or painful story to tell? What beat temperature would you prefer to use? Can you uh, also make it rhyme?

- **FEATURES**: personal diss upon another, transparent sharing of personal failing or imposed problem

# 4

# DESCRIPTION

## HipHopetype #2

| Rejection | Description | Demonstration | Prescription | Aspiration | Recognition |
|---|---|---|---|---|---|
| HipHopetypes Corresponding with Honored Hip Hop Elements | | | | | |
| MC | DJ | Graffiti | Knowledge of Self | B-boy/girl | ALL |
| Unholy Trinity Antidote to the Corresponding Anti-Creative Forces | | | | | |
| FEAR | | | FASCINATION | | |
| exclusion | delusion | marginalization | indecision | desolation | invalidation |
| HipHopetypes Ethos as Evidence of Creative GENIUS | | | | | |
| FAITH | | | FACILITATION | | |
| inclusion | clarity | empowerment | wisdom | optimism | dignity & respect |

# THE PICS KEEP COMING

Rapper Chuck D from the hit 90s group, Public Enemy, once described Hip Hop as the "Black CNN."[1] Meaning, that just like the Cable News Network (CNN) channel that revolutionized cable television with its round-the-clock, twenty-four hour news cycle separate and apart from traditional network news broadcasts, Hip Hop also provided an alternative outlet for news — black news rather — for events happening outside of the white-dominated mainstream.

Chuck D's analogy was especially appropriate given the fact that when Hip Hop began to explode in popularity during the early 1990s, listeners lacked technology to instantaneously connect with one another (e.g., Instagram, YouTube, Twitter or Facebook). Indeed, part of the reason why such current social media outlets have remained so popular is that they often provide a raw, immediate, unfiltered and unmediated form of expression in contrast to images and messaging that is framed through a "mainstream lens."[2] Hip Hop did and still does to a degree, offer this alternate form of unmitigated expression.

In keeping with one of the unofficial mantras of Hip Hop — artists are often praised and regarded for "keeping it real" — meaning, the experience they share is authentic and is not contrived or created for mere entertainment or worse, purely profit-based purposes. To the extent that one is rewarded for their authenticity is one matter — to downright lie is the crime.[3] Perhaps, the focus on "realness" stems from a coping mechanism for many born or trapped within Inner City, USA, where in the absence of other material or social resources, all that one has is their own sense of self and identity.[4] This helps explain why personal offenses and slights are treated with grave solemnity within the proverbial "ghetto."

Tracks within the Description HipHopetype are characterized by vivid portrayals of the lives that people live from the margins. Without this intellectual and emotional space created by Hip Hop music, many (white) Americans simply would not know **THE REALNESS** about the people living in neighborhoods that they seldom get the chance to see or tangibly experience with any depth or consistency. At any rate, in many a Hip Hop track, the author will take the time to paint a complete and accurate picture or describe in painstaking detail the circumstances surrounding their decision-making. Or, the author will describe specific events, trends or phenomena within their neighborhood emblematic of larger systemic issues.

One caveat to this category that must be briefly noted: poetic license is generally granted to artists that tell a story that is not 100% factually true so long as the story is representative of a "real experience."[5] Artists will frequently employ imagination in describing themselves, their exploits or general experiences of someone in the position of a visibly identifiable person of color battling the context or consequences of the Unholy Trinity. Yet, such artists are not penalized if such imaging clearly speaks to an authentic scenario (whether based in fantasy or not) evidently borne about or influenced from inhabiting a world shaped by the overarching forces of Romantic Racialism, Feminitiy or Negrophobia. Here, creative or artistic license may be judiciously employed, but not exploited, akin to when Hollywood states that a media project is "based upon a true story."

Again, the cardinal sin here is if an artist makes a claim that has no relevance or cannot be substantiated. Such scrutiny exists, for, the listener has little else to work with when the artist seeks to figuratively make a "verbal contract" with the listener. The listener gives power, credence or respect to the author's words if deemed worthy of investment. Here, word is literally bond. *Dictum meum pactum.*

# YOU'RE WELCOME

In the ten examples that follow, consider the Unholy Trinity and how it may inform or influence the track profiled. Representative examples of the Description HipHopetype include, but are not limited to:

| CLASSIC Description Example #1 | | | |
|---|---|---|---|
| **Artist** | **Track** | **Sample** | **When** |
| Biggie Smalls | "Juicy" (1994) | "We used to fuss when the landlord dissed us, no heat! Wonder why Christmas missed us. Birthdays was the worst days, now we sip champagne when we're thirstay!" | 3:12 mark |
| **LINK:** https://www.youtube.com/watch?v=4M0ObL56C0A | | | |

**Brief Analysis:** When Biggie Smalls was a small big kid named Christopher Wallace, life was not easy. In contrast to idyllic suburban settings frequently depicted on television and in the movies complete with bucolic landscapes and guaranteed personal needs, Biggie punctuates this rhyme with memories of childhood trauma and tragedy, for lack of a better description. No heat in the winter, while living on the East Coast (as in Brooklyn, New York) clearly makes for an uncomfortable scenario. If a young child cannot "celebrate" Christmas in the American capitalist tradition of receiving gifts, this makes for further misfortune. If the one day of the year where one is to celebrate their existence instead is the "worst day" of the calendar year, Biggie is not making reference to the uncontrollable and unfortunate timing of poor weather on the day in question, but rather is directly referencing a poor socio-economic scenario (pun intended) whereupon such a celebration was stunted or muted by other constraining living conditions.

| Description Example #2 | | | |
|---|---|---|---|
| **Artist** | **Track** | **Sample** | **When** |
| Q-Tip | "In the Sun" (2002)<br><br>by Large Professor (feat. Q-Tip) | "I feel it in my bone — a child's without a home; a prison cell holds the dream to a black teen." | 1:41 mark |
| **LINK:** https://www.youtube.com/watch?v=OOnXezkRKzI | | | |

**Brief Analysis:** Q-tip paints a grim picture. His blanket statement of the prison cell may be more fact than fiction in light of federal statistical data from the Department of Justice that shows young black males are treated more harshly by the system.[6] Black males still account for a third of juvenile court cases, which is grossly disproportionate to their population percentage. One study showed that a black male who committed just five crimes was just as likely to receive facility placement as a young white male who committed forty crimes illustrating the higher probability that black males are less likely to be seen as worthy of rehabilitation but rather, worthy of incarceration.[7]

| Description Example #3 | | | |
|---|---|---|---|
| **Artist** | **Track** | **Sample** | **When** |
| stic.man | "W-4" (2004)<br><br>by Dead Prez | "I done worked over hot a** stoves. I done picked up trash off roads. What you know about being poor?" | 1:27 mark |
| **LINK:** https://www.youtube.com/watch?v=kpGX1b2d1tA | | | |

**Brief Analysis:** The song title cleverly references the Internal Revenue Service document every employee must complete if they wish to be financially compensated or paid. The song is about the invisible struggle against joblessness or low-wage, low quality jobs with hopelessness available to a urban black male. In the selection above, Sticman of the "revolutionary, but gangsta" Hip Hop group Dead Prez provides social commentary while describing a sobering picture of his work history.

| Description Example #4 | | | |
| --- | --- | --- | --- |
| **Artist** | **Track** | **Sample** | **When** |
| Jay Electronica | "Exhibit C" (2009) | "When I was sleeping on the train; Sleeping on Meserole Avenue out in the rain; Without a single slice of pizza to my name; Too proud to beg for change, mastering the pain..." | 0:49 mark |
| **LINK:** https://www.youtube.com/watch?v=qPRl0LzD_MA | | | |

**Brief Analysis:** Jay Electronica starts off the track with this verse, cutting through the pleasantries and getting straight to the point. He struggled as a youth. Period. More importantly, he describes how he suffered and how he dealt with it – by discovering Knowledge of Self through religion: "I ain't believe it then, n*gga I was homeless. Fighting, shootin' dice, smokin' weed on the corners. Tryna find the meaning of life in a Corona; till the Five Percenters rolled up on a n*gga and informed him." The Corona symbolizes the common technique for those afflicted by the Unholy Trinity to "self-medicate" their wounds through drugs and alcohol -- a drug Jay no longer needs now that he has found Allah.

By converting to Islam, Jay found enlightenment through the aid of the "Five Percenters," or grouping of the Nation of Gods and Earths that teach that the true and living God is personified through living black people today. They further organize the world's population in three primary groupings: 85% are shrouded in ignorance and are controlled and manipulated by 10% of the people who are elite, but abuse their knowledge of the truth for personal gain while 5% of the population have true understanding of the existence of both groups, yet are charged with the responsibility to enlighten the others. Jay makes several religious references, describing his religious identity by rapping in Arabic later in the track ("Muhammad A'Salaamaleikum RasoulAllah Subhanahu wa ta'ala" -- Warning! Hot fire!).

## Description Example #6

| Artist | Track | Sample | When |
|---|---|---|---|
| Immortal Technique | "Dance with the Devil" (2001) | "I once knew a n*gga, whose real name was William; his primary concern was making a million..." | 0:21 mark |

**LINK:** https://www.youtube.com/watch?v=qggxTtnKTMo

**Brief Analysis:** While likely a fictional story (at least we hope so), Immortal Technique paints a chilling and perverted picture in describing what the naïve Billy Jacobs does to "make it" in a chilling (and perverted?) society.

The song is supported by a **COOL** beat (sampled by Henry Mancini's "Love Story") to allow for the listener to concentrate on the thick detail that Immortal Technique includes. The song itself is graphic and chilling and likely would never see the light of day on commercial airwaves although the scenario described is ironically likely influenced by collective commercialized messaging from mainstream media transmuted directly through commercial airwaves.

Immortal Technique has not necessarily pioneered this technique, as many Hip Hop artists describe both the "poor" choices that many make whilst trying to navigate outside of the maze of marginalization:

- Cru, "Just Another Case"
- Unknown Prophets, "The Wrong Route"
- KRS-One, "Love's Gonna Get'cha"

In adopting the perspective of one who is closer to the victim, they not only humanize the actors they describe, but they also provide commentary on the limited and even **POORER OPTIONS** the victim had to choose from in the first place. These stories do not exonerate poor decision making, nor do they celebrate an anti-statist position of violating the law or being rebels without a cause. Instead, these descriptive stories illuminate the frail limitations of our personal and collective humanity. Such stories can be, but are not necessarily emblematic of the Prescription HipHopetype (see Chapter 6, *infra*).

## CLASSIC   Description Example #5

| Artist | Track | Sample | When |
|--------|-------|--------|------|
| Grandmaster Flash | "The Message" (1982)<br><br>by Grandmaster Flash & the Furious Five | "Broken glass everywhere! People pissing on the stairs, you know they just don't care. I can't take the smell, can't take the noise; got no money to move out, I guess I got no choice." | 0:43 mark |
| **LINK:** https://www.youtube.com/watch?v=gYMkEMCHtJ4 | | | |

**Brief Analysis:** For those who have not been, Grandmaster Flash lyrically takes listeners on a journey through his neighborhood or the ghetto. The Grandmaster describes social dysfunction in the ghetto, but provides not judgment but insight on the larger institutional constructs that precipitate conditions whereupon these dysfunctional scenarios exist.

This track is also included because it (like Biggie Smalls' "Juicy") is considered a pioneering classic. What does it mean if the description is largely accurate and free from embellishment? What does that mean about life in America? How did the author create this narrative? For further context on from whence came the inspiration, go research pictures of what Inner City, USA looked like in the 1970s when President Jimmy Carter decided to visit the South Bronx (New York).[8]

Often overlooked is the chorus:

> Don't push me, 'cause I'm close to the edge...I'm trying not to lose my head! Huh, huh, huh! It's like a jungle sometimes you know I wonder how I keep from going under.

The chorus is quite revealing of a distressed psychological state; one that borders on the edge of sanity based upon the cumulative effect of various stressors related to the Unholy Trinity.[9]

| CLASSIC | Description Example #7 | | |
|---|---|---|---|
| **Artist** | **Track** | **Sample** | **When** |
| N.W.A. | "F*ck tha Police" (1988) | "F*ck the police coming straight from the underground; a young n*gga got it bad 'cause I'm brown; and not the other color so police think; they have the authority to kill a minority." | 0:30 mark |
| **LINK:** https://www.youtube.com/watch?v=7WiT-c3NA0M | | | |

**Brief Analysis:** "Black CNN" strikes again. This track attracted considerable controversy for what was perceived at the time as rhetoric that was anti-state in tone.

While the track title employs strong language, what may be helpful is analysis of the song's context to see if the title still makes sense. Similar to how the Black Panthers civil rights group was founded as a protectionary response to repeated instances of police brutality within their community, N.W.A. (N*ggaz With Attitudes) created a song in response to what they perceived as consistent, but heavy-handed policing techniques within their neighborhoods.

**NOTE:** Black Panthers, while still harboring a reputation for being "militant," must be placed within proper historical perspective. The Black Panther Party stirred controversy for their rhetoric and imagery of exercising their Second Amendment rights to bear arms, but hardly did so. There are few historical accounts of armed Black Panther members storming into majority white neighborhoods and unleashing their terror. Meanwhile, the opposite did in fact happen. The Ku Klux Klan (KKK), founded immediately after the Civil War to restore "law and order," terrorized black communities routinely with impunity through church bombings, physical attacks, cross burnings and lynchings. KKK membership peaked at four million during the 1920s whereas Black Panther membership peaked at 10,000 during the late 1960s.[10] Why does the Black Panther Party still have a militant and threatening reputation?

| Description Example #8 | | | |
|---|---|---|---|
| **Artist** | **Track** | **Sample** | **When** |
| Magestik Legend | "Million Miles Away" (2010) | "Sister didn't sweat it, my daughter's allergy was sunflower — Father didn't forget it but [I] couldn't remember we even talk 'bout it. A year ago they diagnosed him with Alzheimers, incurable, I had hope till I saw how it made his handsome looks catch up with his age, old; I'm thinking selfish when I'm tellin' him to hang on." | 2:52 mark |
| **LINK:** https://www.youtube.com/watch?v=AiXXrnPhtrQ | | | |

**Brief Analysis:** Of the three verses offered, the third is flat out tear-inducing. The author reveals the painful struggle of losing his father as his father loses his memory to Alzheimer's disease. In a world where relationships between young black males and their fathers are often criticized as being non-existent (see the "Moynihan Report"),[II] the overarching themes of love and affection can be seen and heard from "a million miles away" based upon the clear and poignant picture painted by the author.

The music selection is also **GENIUS** in that it enhances the emotion conveyed through the lyrics, and amplifies a feeling of wistfulness that is difficult to express verbally, but perhaps more easily expressed auditorially. The soft, repetitive, fading echo of the titular phrase "million miles away" after the track's third verse will send any listener off into the deepest recesses of their mind for contemplative thought, and make the grateful listener jump up to hug their closest living parent (if afforded the opportunity) once the track is over.

## Description Example #9

| Artist | Track | Sample | When |
|---|---|---|---|
| Cee Lo Green | "Git Up, Git Out, Git Something" (1994)<br><br>by Outkast feat. Goodie Mob | "I don't recall, ever graduating at all. Sometimes I feel I'm just a disappointment to y'all." | 0:36 mark |
| LINK: https://www.youtube.com/watch?v=Ttk3IUKfn4U | | | |

**Brief Analysis:** Cee Lo Green feels like a failure in life. This overriding sense of social rejection as a result of him not measuring up to established standards of minimal education appear to bother him — especially since this is his opening line of his exposition on why it is nonetheless so important to not give up on the concept of life.

## Description Example #10

| Artist | Track | Sample | When |
|---|---|---|---|
| Ghostface Killah | "Guest House" (2009)<br><br>by Ghostface Killah feat. Fabolous & Shareefa | "Very impatient, I'm getting nervous, can't stop pacing, my heart's racing; her Nextel don't get no service!" | 1:06 mark |
| LINK: https://www.youtube.com/watch?v=vBd2q1KUim8 | | | |

**Brief Analysis:** Ghostface delivers another storytelling gem in relating a story of how he suspected his wife of infidelity and before describing the "drama" that takes place later in the scenario later in the song, sets the scene by initially describing in lucid detail his opulent living conditions and his growing uneasiness with his wife's tardiness over "a gallon of milk." Yet, the storytelling style of Ghostface cannot be overlooked in this instance for it is deceptively difficult to recreate. Ghostface adopts a controlled, conversational tone that nonetheless rhymes and allows for slow building of an otherwise stressful situation. The phone operator bits that both open and conclude the track hint at a second story layering...as in, was the sequence a dream, a joke or not about infidelity at all?
**HINT:** "Bring that big joint..."

# Before You Bounce

- The **Description HipHopetype** speaks to one's attempt to situate themselves within humanity through shared information

- **FEATURES:** creation of voice, rich narrative, consistent thread of personal divulging, creation of voice, rich narrative, consistent thread, personal divulging, detailed storytelling

- **BONUS:** Jean Grae, "My Story" tackles the tough topic of abortion — whether true or false, it rings true and will never see the light of airplay; listen to how this female emcee takes care not to describe her body, but rather, to paint a portrait of her emotions inside her body instead: https://www.youtube.com/watch?v=jFz6ECvaiqQ

- **DOUBLE BONUS:** Blu & Exile's "Dancing with the Rain" track is also descriptive of a mindstate not commonly admitted to by males, let alone males of color; @ the 1:51 mark he specifically references the "taboo" topic of depression: https://www.youtube.com/watch?v=Ml5RhkyKXyc

# 5

# DEMONSTRATION

## HipHopetype #3

| Rejection | Description | Demonstration | Prescription | Aspiration | Recognition |
|-----------|-------------|---------------|--------------|------------|-------------|
| **HipHopetypes Corresponding with Honored Hip Hop Elements** | | | | | |
| MC | DJ | Graffiti | Knowledge of Self | B-boy/girl | ALL |
| **Unholy Trinity Antidote to the Corresponding Anti-Creative Forces** | | | | | |
| FEAR | | | FASCINATION | | |
| exclusion | delusion | marginalization | indecision | desolation | invalidation |
| **HipHopetypes Ethos as Evidence of Creative GENIUS** | | | | | |
| FAITH | | | FACILITATION | | |
| inclusion | clarity | empowerment | wisdom | optimism | dignity & respect |

# THE TRICKS KEEP COMING

America in theory, is about many things: freedom, justice & equality to name a few off the top. In practice, three other concepts receive an inordinate amount of attention within mainstream media and culture, namely: sex, money & power. These three realms likely should be re-labeled as the "American Dream Triple Team" as these themes have been constant throughout American History and consistently attract significant attention within mainstream media.[1]

| American Dream Triple Team | | |
|---|---|---|
| Sex | Money | Power |

While it would be unfair to essentialize and presume that all who inhabit the capitalist society called America are driven by the three concepts of sex, money & power, **MANY INDEED ARE**. Without wading into another "chicken & egg" argument over whether society is driven by these motivators and seeks it out in media or whether media produces and reproduces these themes, thereby engendering demand, for our analysis many print advertisements, commercials, television shows and movies feature these concepts widely.

It follows that for marginalized individuals, sex, money & power would equally appeal as evidence of societal value and social progress. In keeping with the American Dream Triple Team, this HipHopetype speaks most directly to **POWER**; as Demonstration references a literal or figurative demonstration of one's power or potential power, whether it be sexual, economic or social in nature. Such a demonstration is a powerful declaration and appeal of one's humanity to whoever will listen. The listener validates the author's humanity by acknowledging the author's presence on the planet via their demonstration.

# DEBUNKING BRAGGADOCIO

Sorry.

When MCs within Hip Hop describe emphatically their accomplishments or potential for greatness, something more than mere "braggadocio" is taking place. Braggadocio is a disparaging term used by mainstream media to criticize those within Rap Music who appear to be obsessed in only talking about themselves.[2] In actuality, such declarations are an evidence-based methodology to demonstrate one's presence, place and purchase in life (otherwise know as value). In other words, Demonstration techniques can also be read as appeals to humanity for democracy, dignity and respect. Criticized by mainstream media as evidence of the solipsistic, narcissistic MC, in actuality, Demonstration is actually an important and clever way to evidence one's humanity. In other words, by describing one's humanity within terms that exceed or stretch the bounds of normal humanity, the raconteur is proclaiming their existence in a very public way so that they may be recognized and respected.

This makes perfect sense when considering the first HipHopetype of Rejection which characterizes the narrative of so many black and brown MCs. Many people of color inherit well-documented narratives of forced assimilation and marginalization that raising up one's own voice to be heard is a significant act of self-realization. After all, whites are unashamed in trumpeting their successes in life to excess. We have museums, statutes, buildings and shrines which constantly remind us of their achievements within this capitalistic mainstream society. But this is considered normal. It is simply part and parcel of how our society is constructed. Yet, when a minority, let alone a minority male voice rises up, it is regarded differently.[3]

The two principal ways Demonstration manifests itself is through Craft and Conquest. Again, with the forces of the Unholy Trinity as an overriding influential force on the psychological and social makeup and development of the majority of Hip Hop artists, most of whom are black and brown males who are connected in some way, shape or form to "the struggle" against marginalization and invalidation, it is not difficult to see how demonstrating one's power would become a common theme. With both the Craft and Conquest strands, the commonality linking the two is the ability to exert control and mastery over one's domain — something that is not easily done in the "real world" outside of the Hip Hop multi-verse.

## Craft

What better way to demonstrate one's dedication and fealty to Hip Hop than by illustrating a new innovation (or discovery) that expands the growing Hip Hop multi-verse even further? Just like scientists and academics gather at annual conferences and congratulate each other for new articles or manuscripts that investigate or flesh out new nuances within the field, these demonstrations within Hip Hop circles are no different.

Craft Demonstrations are typically reserved for those who indulge in the "art of the rhyme," and therefore employ new techniques; groundbreaking styles, complex, complicated and difficult rhyme schemes, controversial themes, mind-bending wordplay, captivating storytelling or cogent and concise social commentary as a demonstration of personal skill or knowledge about Hip Hop. If the listener walks away saying "Wow!" then the author has succeeded with their demonstration of power. Such demonstrations serve notice to the listener that: 1) the author is a talented individual that the listener should take seriously and 2) the author is serious about Hip Hop.

## Conquest

Conquest Demonstrations illustrate the author's power through past accomplishments or projected accomplishments. Often, such accomplishments may include tales involving (wait for it...) sex, money & power. Sexual conquest is not only important to virtually every mainstream movie storyline, but it is also important to the marginalized author seeking to demonstrate that they too, are desirable and are wanted by others (although this unchecked desire can easily lead down the path of misogyny). High economic achievement is virtually self-explanatory within our capitalistic society. The last prong of power is fascinating, for many of the authors lack "power" within any "official" mainstream capacity. Meaning, the overwhelming majority of Hip Hop authors, as members of a marginalized class, are not likely to hold national or local political office or do not own and operate business enterprises employing significant numbers of individuals akin to those listed on the latest "Fortune 500" listing.[4] While lacking institutionalized power within media, education, commerce, politics, etc., many authors nonetheless are not powerless and demonstrate their prowess through tales recounting their ability to mitigate violence against unsuspecting individuals who chose (unwisely) to "test" the author on an individual basis.

The superficial criticism of such remonstrations is that Hip Hop is thereby violent. A closer look may reveal that there is more than what meets the ear. Dr. Henry Louis Gates, Chair of Africana Studies at Harvard University, has written extensively about the "signifying monkey,"[5] which encapsulates the concept that within the African American community, males will often "bluff" violence through premeditated and calculated demonstrations of violence to ironically intimidate the other so that true violence can be avoided altogether.

Hence, when a Hip Hop emcee waxes on about how they did "such and such" to "so and so" or how they will do so if someone foolishly decides to impinge upon their personal space or character, it is not necessarily a glorification of violence as much as it is a cleverly disguised plea for peace — peace upon the author who ultimately is under stress and wishes not to be perturbed further. When an author therefore proclaims that they are "doing big thangs," or that they "are in da building," they are announcing their presence and instructing the listener to recognize them as an individual of power. The job is on you as the listener to determine whether speaker is bluffing or not!

# THINKING DIFFERENT

Additionally, it should not be overlooked, that as a demonstration of the Hip Hop artist's power to think freely, notice how many words are purposely misspelled — well, at least misspelled according to conventional rules of English. We all learned early that "English is not a phonetic language." So, when the artist Redman spells the word "action" as "aksion" on the track "Time 4 Sum Aksion," is he effectively exposing himself as an uneducated individual who cannot comply to existing rules of grammar? Or is he a forward-thinking pragmatist, who visually made the spelling of the word more easily align with its phonetic rendering, thereby evidencing himself as an innovative individual who chooses not to conform to existing rules of grammar as a small, but subtle act of deliberate resistance? For whatever it's worth, in looking up the word "action" at www.dictionary.com, the phonetic, parenthetical rendering is (ak-sh*uh*-n). Also, consider Redman's rendering of "4 Sum" as opposed to spelling out "for some" which thereby accentuates the mathematical implication of connecting the concepts "time" and "aksion" by rewriting "4 Sum" even though as hominyms they sound *exactly the same*.

# NOM DE GUERRE

For those of us who do not speak the French language, *nom de guerre* means pseudonym, but specifically is a name under which one expresses themselves, whether it be politically or artistically, as with many of the stage names that many Hip Hop MCs adopt when performing. The vast array of different MC names likely requires a book unto itself. But for now, such names we presume are purposed, conscious choices that represents an idea or image the artist wishes to convey. Often, these names are far from deprecating and are quite self-congratulatory, likely in dialogue with the Unholy Trinity that presumes incompetence. These names are a form of Demonstration in showing the world that this individual is a force to be reckoned with; that they exist. Given this idea, what do these "stage names" tell us?

| | |
|---|---|
| LL Cool J (Ladies Love Cool James) | Large Professor |
| GURU (Gifted Unlimited Rhymes Universal) | Royce, da 5'9" Wonder |
| KRS-One (Knowledge Reigns Supreme Over Nearly Everyone) | Prodigy |

# YOU'RE WELCOME

In the ten examples that follow, consider the Unholy Trinity and how it may inform or influence the track profiled. Representative examples of the Demonstration HipHopetype include, but are not limited to:

| CLASSIC Demonstration Example #1 | | | |
|---|---|---|---|
| **Artist** | **Track** | **Sample** | **When** |
| Biggie Smalls | "Juicy" (1994) | "Phone bill about $2Gs flat! No need to worry, my accountant handles that." | 2:52 mark |
| **LINK:** https://www.youtube.com/watch?v=4M0ObL56C0A | | | |

**Brief Analysis:** While informing the listener about his "humble beginnings" within the inner city, Anti-Horatio, ghetto environment, Biggie also demonstrates for the listener his personal prowess in overcoming past problems by alerting our attention to his new "problem" of a hefty phone bill. This can be easily confused as glamorization of material culture and the blinding love for money, however, when placed within proper context, this is a declarative demonstration of personal power to conquer a challenging period in one's life and persist and persevere as victorious. Horatio Alger would be proud.

## CLASSIC Demonstration Example #2

| Artist | Track | Sample | When |
|---|---|---|---|
| Bizmarkie | "A One Two" (1986) | "I'd like to introduce myself..." | entire track |
| LINK: https://www.youtube.com/watch?v=r8Vni__Be2M | | | |

**Brief Analysis:** Whereas Biggie Smalls demonstrated his personal prowess, via conquest, here, Bizmarkie demonstrates his personal prowess through craft. Bizmarkie is the sole source of soul streaming through the listener's speakers for this track. Bizmarkie is going "acapella," meaning no other formal instrument other than his body and his mouth are employed. Regardless of whether you are an ardent supporter of Hip Hop or not, it truly is a marvel to listen to a human being create a cacophony of sound in what appears to be uninterrupted **GENIUS**, meaning that it was not edited, spliced or mixed together to create the resulting impressive effect.

## Demonstration Example #3

| Artist | Track | Sample | When |
|---|---|---|---|
| Gift of Gab | "Alphabet Aerobics" (1999) by Blackalicious | "Artificial amateurs, aren't it all amazing; analytically I assault, animate things" | entire track |
| LINK: https://www.youtube.com/watch?v=rYzBSKluxtI | | | |

**Brief Analysis:** Tim Bradley in "The Poetics of Hip Hop"[6] argues that Hip Hop lyricism can be read like poetry and therefore can be appreciated on a higher intellectual plane as a result. Well, the direct intellectual connection to poetry is not necessary in order to appreciate how artistic and difficult some rhymes can be. Here, Blackalicious demonstrates his intellectual prowess by composing an entire song using every letter in the alphabet. His original idea is made more exquisite in that for each letter, he rhymes using several words that also start with the same letter (i.e., alliteration). The track also starts at a slow tempo and increases in speed up until the end. Listen to the track and then see if you can "sing along...."

## Demonstration Example #4

| Artist | Track | Sample | When |
|---|---|---|---|
| Supernatural | "MC Juice & Supernatural Freestyle Session" (1999) | "You can't think that! Yo brother, I'm reading the sign -- I'm looking inside of your eyes and I'm reading your mind..." | 2:47 mark |
| **LINK:** https://www.youtube.com/watch?v=8YCVzgod_wU |||||
| **BONUS:** part of what makes Dr. Martin Luther King's "I Have a Dream" speech special is that it is said he spoke "extemporaneously" towards the end. How different is this from freestyling? |||||

**Brief Analysis:** This underground freestyling legend at least on this track defies common logic and convention. For starters, very few can competently engage the art of freestyle, or the free association of words while keeping pace with a rhythmic beat. When we say free association, the idea is to not rehash a premeditated, prepared statement but to make oneself vulnerable to mistake, error and failure by spontaneously and extemporaneously putting together prose that should not only be clear and cogent to the listener, but should also be witty and uh, also rhyme too! If this sounds difficult, it is only because it is. MC Supernatural takes matters to the next level by freestyling in not one, but in two split personalities — going so far as to change his voice, content, tenor and themes all on the fly. This feat is nothing short of mind-boggling and awe-inspiring. MC Supernatural reminds us of Harvard University Professor Howard Gardner's theory about multiple intelligences[7] and that when done properly, freestyling within Hip Hop represents a different type of intelligence that few among us can emulate, let alone approach.

## Demonstration Example #5

| Artist | Track | Sample | When |
|---|---|---|---|
| Nas | "Rewind" (2001) | "Dog whatever they call you, God just listen; I spit a story backwards, it starts at the ending..." | entire track |
| LINK: https://www.youtube.com/watch?v=unpNsXFNTVA ||||

**Brief Analysis:** Nas has already through a lengthy and wide-ranging career demonstrated his ability to engage the craft. Yet with this track, he tells a story backwards. Backwards. The previous sentences are trying to convey to you the reader that Nas composed a track backwards. As in the opposite of forward. Backwards. This feat is so impressive, it is almost insulting. Try listening to the track first before looking at the video. If you love decoding puzzles or intricate patterns, try this one on for size.

## Demonstration Example #6

| Artist | Track | Sample | When |
|---|---|---|---|
| Edan | "Emcees Smoke Crack" (2002) | "Geometric poop — get your sh*t straight; dictionary director, that means I dictate." | 0:25 mark |
| LINK: https://www.youtube.com/watch?v=B1ZZOIg30Y4 ||||

**Brief Analysis:** This Demonstration Hiphopetype is arguably the most inspiring to observe as there are indeed a plethora of examples wherein artists communicate their love for Hip Hop through skill. Here, Edan is no slouch on the mic and inspires questions as to how many Ph.D.s he personally could attain within a rich academic career given the fact that he likely would have scored high on his Graduate Record Examination verbal portion. Listening to the first sixty seconds of this track is akin to Alice gazing lustily through "the looking glass" and falling down the rabbit hole — Edan clearly utilizes an "abstract" rhyme style that is initially difficult to follow. Yet, once attuned, the lucid alliteration, loquacious word play and linguistic gymnastics are quite admirable.

## Demonstration Example #7

| Artist | Track | Sample | When |
|---|---|---|---|
| One Be Lo | "Reality Check" (2000) <br><br> by Binary Star | "Honestly my number one policy is quality — never sell my soul is my philosophy." | 1:25 mark |
| LINK: https://www.youtube.com/watch?v=F8IzlbDTgNM | | | |

**Brief Analysis:** The expression and communication of Binary Star's cultural values through the content of their rhymes publicly demonstrates that Binary Star is serious about taking Hip Hop serious. Honor thy craft.

## Demonstration Example #8

| Artist | Track | Sample | When |
|---|---|---|---|
| Mos Def (Yasiin Bey) | "Two Words" (2004) <br><br> by Kanye West feat. Mos Def & Freeway | "Two words, United States, no love, no breaks, low brow, high stakes..." | 0:38 mark |
| LINK: https://www.youtube.com/watch?v=tkFOBx6j0l8 | | | |

**Brief Analysis:** This duet between Mos Def and Kanye West (pre-Kardashian) demonstrates skill in a novel way. Here, the "game within the game" is to convey larger concepts by using a series of smaller concepts commonly expressed in two words. Not easy. At all. Try it. You'll see (Wait! Is "you'll see" actually three words? Darn!).

## Demonstration Example #9

| Artist | Track | Sample | When |
|---|---|---|---|
| Heltah Skeltah & O.G.C. (Originoo Gunn Clappaz) | "Laflaur Leflah Eshkoshka" (1996) <br><br> by Heltah Skeltah & O.G.C. | "OGC, Heltah Skeltah be the best y'all; Fab 5 slam from East to West y'all..." | 0:14 mark |
| LINK: https://www.youtube.com/watch?v=i4sW3jJuVDg | | | |

**Brief Analysis:** These five individuals from Brownsville, Brooklyn, New York are definitely Demonstrating lyrical prowess here through clever word plays and assonance techniques. Also, on display is the group unity they will exercise with impunity upon the poor unsuspecting individual who thinks that he can disrupt their "vibe," or attempt to insert negativity in their circle of friendship, utilizing "abstract" style of word association.

| Demonstration Example #10 | | | |
|---|---|---|---|
| **Artist** | **Track** | **Sample** | **When** |
| Vinny Paz | "Ghengis Khan" (2000) <br><br> by Jedi Mind Tricks feat. Tragedy Khadafi | "5'9", tatted up, mad stocky — animal thug who bust slugs in the lobby! | 1:45 mark |
| **LINK:** https://www.youtube.com/watch?v=bGTRgV2thac | | | |

**Brief Analysis:** Philadelphia white Italian rapper Vinny Paz's quote signifies or demonstrates how "hardcore" he is. Not having any reservation over firing a loaded weapon within a public space hints strongly that he is thinking different and is not restricted by conventional middle class norms. Whether factual or fictional, the image now exists. The problem is, if he is bluffing, are you going to "test" him to find out?

# BEFORE YOU BOUNCE

- The **Demonstration HipHopetype** speaks to one's sense of power and the tangible or imagined manifestations thereof

- **FEATURES:** tangible display of humanity through craft and conquest

- **BONUS:** Hmmm! Deliciously difficult: http://www.youtube.com/watch?v=Teaft0Kg-Ok

# 6

# PRESCRIPTION

## HipHopetype #4

| Rejection | Description | Demonstration | Prescription | Aspiration | Recognition |
|---|---|---|---|---|---|
| **HipHopetypes Corresponding with Honored Hip Hop Elements** | | | | | |
| MC | DJ | Graffiti | Knowledge of Self | B-boy/girl | ALL |
| **Unholy Trinity Antidote to the Corresponding Anti-Creative Forces** | | | | | |
| **FEAR** | | | **FASCINATION** | | |
| exclusion | delusion | marginalization | indecision | desolation | invalidation |
| **HipHopetypes Ethos as Evidence of Creative GENIUS** | | | | | |
| **FAITH** | | | **FACILITATION** | | |
| inclusion | clarity | empowerment | wisdom | optimism | dignity & respect |

# THE WITS KEEP COMING

Every living creature must struggle for survival.

Survival is difficult.

Thus, to complete our sentence-long syllogism, it is no surprise that it takes at least twelve years of schooling to "learn" how to live and cope within society.

Surviving within a system rife with destructive manifestations of the Unholy Trinity is especially difficult.[1] Thus, when confronted on a daily basis with the friction of such anti-creative forces, many find it difficult to overcome the inertia of presumed incompetence and find major success without the use of extralegal means. Sure, one can "study" their way out the ghetto, but the statistics and data indicate that such a route is not easy, automatic nor guaranteed. Just like white collar criminals, many marginalized youth fall prey to the allure of quick gains (in the absence of other practically viable options) and therefore sucumb to a life of crime. Many others believe that they can dribble or rap their way out of the ghetto. For the rest of us, the question becomes, "what to do?" How should individuals deal with one's personal ambitions for improvement versus society's restrictions on such movement?

To answer such questions of social import, it is customary for individuals to seek out wise counsel or advice when in need of an additional perspective. If one knows where to look (or listen), above the critiques of violent, misogynistic and materialistic rap music, much of Hip Hop offers valuable advice on how to cope with society and the adopting and evolving face of the Unholy Trinity.

In other words, many Hip Hop artists frequently (not necessarily freely) offer prescriptive advice on a wide range of topics to assist the listener on their quest for survival at the very minimum, or even better, for self-improvement ideally. This technique is novel, for if the individual is the atomic core of any community, the improvement of the individual correlates with the improvement of the family which is the building block of a larger community, and so forth.

Prescriptive advice ranges from insight over what to do when faced with certain scenarios to cautionary tales laden with discouraging warnings over what not to do with one's time, money or energy. Ever cognizant of the largely independent-minded Hip Hop listening base, very rarely will an emcee tell listeners what to do with their life directly in the form of a command. What has proven more effective has been the sharing of personal experiences or stories from which listeners can draw their own conclusions. Accordingly, many Prescription HipHopetypes exhibit characteristics consistent with Description.

After all, if the speed of light explained through the video game *Minecraft*,[2] why not dispense life lessons through Hip Hop? Hence when the Texas based Hip Hop troupe Geto Boys inform the listener in the song "G Code" that "We don't talk to police!" the question is whether they are adopting an anti-state perspective or are subtly dispensing practical advice to distrustful, hurt members of a marginalized community?

# YOU'RE WELCOME

In the ten examples that follow, consider the Unholy Trinity and how it may inform or influence the track profiled. Representative examples of the Presecription HipHopetype include, but are not limited to:

| CLASSIC Prescription Example #1 | | | |
|---|---|---|---|
| **Artist** | **Track** | **Sample** | **When** |
| Biggie Smalls | "Juicy" (1994) | "I made the change from a common thief, to up close and personal with Robin Leach; and I'm far from cheap, I smoke with my peeps all day, spread love — it's the Brooklyn way..." | 1:31 mark |
| **LINK:** https://www.youtube.com/watch?v=4M0ObL56C0A | | | |

**Brief Analysis:** First, let's not overlook the masterful lyricsm as evidenced through the assonance (several words with the same sound) with thief/Leach/cheap/peeps — many of us may not think to sit down and write these words down as rhyming together. Robin Leach was a British host of a famous television show in the late 1980's and early 1990's entitled "Lifestyles of the Rich & Famous." The show presaged subsequent shows such as "MTV Cribs" wherein well-known celebrities would have the chance to proudly display the opulence that their hard earned labors earned them. Hence, Biggie recounts a remarkable Horatio Alger narrative where we goes from a life of crime to a life that's divine.

More importantly, in recounting this remarkable narrative, Biggie dispenses generous advice on how to handle fame for the also-aspiring listener; namely to remain humble and generous if the opportunity presents itself. Even though Biggie has found fortune, he still finds time to maintain his original connection with his "peeps," or people that he used to know when his financial condition was less fortunate. Biggie literally puts his money where his mouth is by spending unabashedly for "skunk," or the recreational drug of marijuana as a way to enjoy life and "spread love" with his friends rather than hoard his newfound resources to himself. The video accompanying this track illustrates Biggie's orientation towards sharing what he has with others.

| Prescription Example #2 | | | |
|---|---|---|---|
| **Artist** | **Track** | **Sample** | **When** |
| Solitair | "Easy to Slip" (2002) | "I had a cousin named Derrick, he hustled on the block. That n*gga was a thug — I was not. Fourteen years old, I watched him; he was the man that I wanted to be — and he was barely sixteen." | 0:40 mark |
| **LINK:** https://www.youtube.com/watch?v=l6VoygloCOo | | | |

**Brief Analysis:** This song employs the "cautionary tale" technique to inform the listener of "Derrick," a real or fictional character to whom many listeners can relate as well as the poor choices Derrick made as a youth in order to pursue a life of prosperity. The sample line chosen above is quite revealing, for it speaks to the pain and dysfunction caused by broken families within impoverished environments and more importantly, how the lack of family structural support can open the door to youth like Derrick making questionable decisions. The line is also acerbic and ironic, for it reveals how through the wide eyes of a fourteen year older, the actions of Derrick loomed large in his mind.

The author accentuates this dynamic by calling his cousing "the man that I wanted to be" even though the listener knows all too well that Derrick was a misguided youth also in need of love and direction as a sixteen year old teenager "coming of age."[3] The narrator hints at his willingness to follow in Derrick's footsteps, thereby exposing his own vulnerability and perhaps that of the listener. Rather than this story being filed away as an exception to the rule, by placing himself closer to Derrick's sphere of influence, the author successfully describes a common scenario of peer pressure that many youth in inner cities face — and unfortunately sucumb to more often than what many would like to admit.

| Prescription Example #3 | | | |
|---|---|---|---|
| **Artist** | **Track** | **Sample** | **When** |
| Pretty Ugly | "Josephine" (2006)<br><br>by Hi Tek (feat. Ghostface Killah, Pretty Ugly & Willie Cottrell Band) | "Years went past before I seen her again; now she slim, but I don't think she'd been in a gym. So I asked her how she been and said I'm done with the men, now I'm saved but I caught AIDS when I was f*cking with them." | 3:26 mark |
| **LINK:** https://www.youtube.com/watch?v=LVZ5nbPDfnA | | | |

**Brief Analysis:** This track is a cautionary tale on two levels. First, Pretty Ugly details how Josephine was not interested in his romance when they first met as she was into the "drug life." This track positions the drug life as an attempt to self-medicate against the confusing and painful undiagnosed symptoms of the Unholy Trinity.

While an alternative is not necessarily offered, it is nonetheless implied that choosing the "drug life" is not the best option. For, while drugs are said to offer temporary relief and escape from reality, they seldom alter the reality outside of the user's direct experience. Here in this message is buried a subtle seed of hope. Despite of or rather, *in spite of* the existence of the Unholy Trinity, the author implies that staying sober enough to confront the realities of life and deal with them in their true and real form is the essence of life. The facilitation and encouragement of the creative energies necessary to proceed with life outside of drugs is **GENIUS**.

Secondly, this track, as composed by males, offers indirect, cautionary advice for its majority-male audience to avoid potential (female) partners that have their priorities confused due to a life of drugs. The selected sample line above reveals that Josephine is now suffering from the AIDS virus and has lost weight as a result of preventable consequences had she made better life decisions.

| Prescription Example #4 | | | |
|---|---|---|---|
| **Artist** | **Track** | **Sample** | **When** |
| Ghostface Killah | "Run" (2004)<br><br>by Ghostface Killah feat. Jadakiss & Comp | "Run! They amp sh*t, plant sh*t, destroy evidence; f*ck a case, I'm not comin' home with no fifty six; die with the heart of Scarface and take fifty licks; before I let these crackers throw me in sh*t." | 1:15 mark |
| **LINK:** https://www.youtube.com/watch?v=eMSY3zfLxRA | | | |

**Brief Analysis:** Both Ghostface and Jadakiss describe in harrowing detail what their life is like on the run from the legal authorities. More importantly, the careful listener will hear the author's commentary on the stressful life of a drug dealer within the inner city — it is not described or depicted as glamorous in any fashion here — it is a hard-scrabble picture shaped by the difficult environment surrounding gainful employment generally made challenging by the Unholy Trinity. Consider Jadakiss's recount @ the 2:56 mark: "Now I'm trying to hold my hammer up, and my pants too; if they don't kill me, they gon' give me a number I can't do; rather it be the streets, than jail where I die at; and I'm asthmatic, so I'm looking for somewhere to hide at."

Now with the challenging task of survival made more complex through the personal choice to engage in the trade of "street pharmaceuticals" (i.e., drug dealing) -- especially within the chorus -- Ghostface et al prescribe what one should do if they wish to stay alive and "successful."

Ghostface implies with the selected line above that young black males are justified in "running" from the cops upon sight since chances are high that the interaction between a white cop and a black male will yield questionable results in the true eyes of justice. Ghostface is very clear on seeing his predicament as a result of pre-existing racial tensions ("before I let these crackers throw me in sh*t"). Without much time to dialogue about the matter, Ghostface simply opts to run and recommends the listener take heed as well.[4]

## Prescription Example #5

| Artist | Track | Sample | When |
|---|---|---|---|
| Mr. SOS | "Earth Essence" (2004)<br><br>CunninLynguists feat. Mr. SOS | "So when what goes up comes down, don't blame it on gravity cause humans have the ability to create; but most of 'em just take, it's so easy to hate." | 1:10 mark |
| **LINK:** https://www.youtube.com/watch?v=OoctWrg2wf8 | | | |

**Brief Analysis:** Mr. SOS uses fantasy within the second verse to have the listener consider what the Earth would actually communicate if it possessed his body to speak. Upon speaking, Mr. SOS describes a world that sounds dystopian in its function — where people kill, steal and conceal from others the higher principles and blessings of life. The listener is then forced to reconcile whether the world described in verse resembles the world the listener currently inhabits. Late in the second verse Mr. SOS drops these gems:

> It took violence to pull together USA again
> What's it gonna take to pull the world together? Aliens
> Attacking or maybe even meteorites
> To make us understand that it's not us that we need to fight
> Whoa...

Mr. SOS takes a laundry list of human failings he detailed up until this point in the track and within a couple of deft strokes of his pen, places them in global perspective. Man's inhumanity to man makes less sense when placed in a universal context of there (currently) being only one planet we know with life. Mr. SOS invites listeners to engage critical thinking to answer the philosophical query of whether the outside presence of a common enemy can reduce the temptation to create enemies amongst each other as members of (wait for it...) the all uniting *human race*.

Finally, Mr. SOS recommends to the listener conduct that will contribute towards a greener, healthier solution — from his perspective at least.

| Prescription Example #6 | | | |
|---|---|---|---|
| **Artist** | **Track** | **Sample** | **When** |
| J-Live | "Money Matters" (2014) | "Paper gotta circulate just to keep the water flushing, stove hot, fridge cold; cabinets full, clothes clean, quarters for the wash and fold; kids grow bigger so the gear grow tight and old; inflation triggers so the prices grow." | 0:29 mark |
| **LINK:** https://www.youtube.com/watch?v=L7fYiUpih1c | | | |

**Brief Analysis:** Here, J-Live describes the general financial difficulty that has faced so many of the non-white, inner city experience. Historical data informs that while African American had to compete with everyone else fair and square upon moving to the large, major metropolises during the Great Migration during World War II, such competition was in many ways restricted. Many labor unions flat out refused blacks as members, rampant discrimination within the private sector and well-meaning but toothless anti-discriminatory measures within the public sector all contributed to a picture wherein black workers generally were the last hired, but the first fired and while on the job, suffered from lower wages and slower promotion rates.

Such conditions add up to a financially disadvantaged picture, especially in contrast to those (as in, white immigrants or middle class laborers) who have done respectably or remarkably financially, and have been able to conserve such momentum with various inheritance laws.

We say all this to say that J-Live's skeptical analysis of simply working hard to become financially successful is likely informed by his understanding of the Unholy Trinity and the ways in which it has worked to keep blacks from working legitimately to obtain the American Dream — outside of a sports/entertainment paradigm.

## CLASSIC Prescription Example #7

| Artist | Track | Sample | When |
|---|---|---|---|
| Lauryn Hill | "Doo Wop (That Thing)" (1998) | "It's silly when girls sell their souls because it's in; look at where you be in, hair weaves like Europeans, fake nails done by Koreans, come again." | 1:21 mark |
| LINK: https://www.youtube.com/watch?v=T6QKqFPRZSA | | | |

**Brief Analysis:** The effervescent Lauryn Hill prescribes conduct becoming of a prideful individual. Her two verses are dedicated to both male and female genders and are aimed at getting people to think critically about the small but significant choices that they make on a daily basis. The National Recording Registry agrees, since Ms. Hill's album containing "Doo Wop" — "The Miseducation of Lauryn Hill" is being entered into the Library of Congress.[5]

## Prescription Example #8

| Artist | Track | Sample | When |
|---|---|---|---|
| The Globetroddas | "Love" (2004) | "Maybe that long talk, firm hug or that laugh will help him read fluently [and perform] better at math." | 0:43 mark |
| LINK: https://www.youtube.com/watch?v=NblC5LA3ylE | | | |

**Brief Analysis:** The second verse almost reads like a laundry list of what one should do to avoid turmoil and find success within their life. Yet, the first verse is quite compassionate in dispensing advice to strangers without insulting the listener, striking the balance with an empathetic tone that would encourage the listener to internalize and act upon the author's message. As much as "love" is bandied about as a topic in many commercial songs, here, the author takes the concept of love literally, and beyond superficial, lust-based associations towards the communal *agape*.

## Prescription Example #9

| Artist | Track | Sample | When |
|--------|-------|--------|------|
| Large Professor | "Stay Chisel" (2002)<br><br>Large Pro feat. Nas | "Kid tried to front so I showed him straight up; had his whole clique flabbergasted; way I was cuttin' him up, one kid yelled out 'Grab the Bastard!' -- tried to rush me, luckily I wasn't rusty; pulled out, served 'em all up like a custy." | 1:58 mark |
| LINK: https://www.youtube.com/watch?v=YtDrXUx5yI8 | | | |

**Brief Analysis:** The Large Professor gives advice on how to survive potentially dangerous scenarios by recounting his personal narrative on how he was ambushed by several individuals with plans to do him harm. However, because he "stayed chiseled," and was physically and emotionally sharp and ready, he was not "rusty" and was able to do what he had to do to merge victorious or alive. **NOTE:** "like a custy" refers to a custard ice cream cone.

## CLASSIC Prescription Example #10

| Artist | Track | Sample | When |
|--------|-------|--------|------|
| Slick Rick | "Children's Story" (1988) | "This ain't funny, so don't you dare laugh; just another case about the wrong path..." | 2:35 mark |
| LINK: https://www.youtube.com/watch?v=HjNTu8jdukA | | | |
| BONUS: https://www.youtube.com/watch?v=ea-ezolZq5k | | | |

**Brief Analysis:** Slick Rick utilizes a direct, linear style to describe a cautionary tale of a young man who chose the "wrong path." Again, the unspoken, driving impetus behind this young man's actions are the structural limitations and restrictions of the Unholy Trinity that deludes a young, urban youth from the inner city into believing that his only way to "make it" in society was to turn to a life of crime as a way to salve a future life trajectory that was essentially hopeless.

**BONUS:** Slick Rick decided to be even more explicit on this track, "Hey Young World" (from the same album as "Children's Story") in providing adolescent youth timeless advice on how best to conduct and comport themselves within the society that they will eventually inherit! "Get ahead...and accomplish things; you'll see the wonder and the joy life brings; don't admire thieves...hey, they don't admire you; their time's limited, hardrocks too. So listen, be strong, scream whoopee-doo; go for yours, 'cause dreams come true." Good advice indeed -- **WHOOPEE-DOO!**

## Before You Bounce

- The **Prescription HipHopetype** speaks to ever-eternal quest for wisdom, as wisdom is the key to a safe and sane survival on this planet

- **FEATURES:** cautionary tale, warning(s) to listener, specific advice, kick knowledge (Knowledge of Self element)

- **BONUS:** consider what might be the Prescription in this straightforward GZA track, "Basic Instructions Before Leaving Earth"? https://www.youtube.com/watch?v=NKpIkOXgAmg

# 7

# ASPIRATION

## HipHopetype #5

| Rejection | Description | Demonstration | Prescription | Aspiration | Recognition |
|---|---|---|---|---|---|
| **HipHopetypes Corresponding with Honored Hip Hop Elements** | | | | | |
| MC | DJ | Graffiti | Knowledge of Self | B-boy/girl | ALL |
| **Unholy Trinity Antidote to the Corresponding Anti-Creative Forces** | | | | | |
| **FEAR** | | | **FASCINATION** | | |
| exclusion | delusion | marginalization | indecision | desolation | invalidation |
| **HipHopetypes Ethos as Evidence of Creative GENIUS** | | | | | |
| **FAITH** | | | **FACILITATION** | | |
| inclusion | clarity | empowerment | wisdom | optimism | dignity & respect |

# THE WHIPS KEEP COMING

Simply describing and ruminating upon one's financially impoverished condition will eventually become depressing and destructive for one's psyche. In keeping with the premise that GENIUS represents creative forces, then spending time talking about how one supercedes destructive forces through creativity makes logical sense.

Enter the Aspiration HipHopetype. Similar to Demonstration, it follows that the three primary areas where Hip Hop artists delve into fantasy or Aspiration are in the realms of the three pillars of American Capitalism: Sex, Money and Power.

| American Dream Triple Team | | |
| :---: | :---: | :---: |
| Sex | Money | Power |

Corrupt, high-ranking politicians embroiled in sexual scandals who use money to cover their tracks is instant news in any part of the country. Most especially, when that friendly politician from Arkansas became the nation's FORTY-SECOND PRESIDENT of the United States of America.[1] But impeached president's aside, any local supermarket checkout counter and its magazine selection will verify our society's fascination with sex, money and power. If anything, we should just ask Hollywood![2] Thus, it is important to recall that these three realms exist and have existed before Hip Hop was ever contemplated.

Who does not want to have fun and feel free and feel good? Exploring one's sexuality is important — especially to the youth coming of age. But while acceptable for whites to partake in "coming of age" experiences, sexuality expressed by blacks has always been viewed more negatively (Negrophobia, i.e., "negro as beast").[3]

With this Hiphopetype, authors will frequently speak in future terms about items they wish to acquire, events they wish to transpire or preferred scenarios that they admire. Often, this fantasy projection results in a reference to one or all of the American Dream Triple Team. Yet, this Hiphopetype must be distinguished from the more commercialized Rap Music that appears to promote similar goals. The steady stream of misogynistic and materialistic references made within Rap Music are different from the more nuanced references in Hip Hop that focus upon the personal experience of these items for larger meaning or collective gain.

Due to the fact that many authors of Hip Hop rhymes are indeed black males, there are two threshold issues to consider: 1) that black males are acutely affected by the Unholy Trinity and as a result, constantly seek to compensate for such constriction and powerlessness, however real or imagined, 2) that since black males are the primary authors of Hip Hop lyrical landscapes, criticism of Hip Hop — however valid — must be mediated through the lens that for whatever reason, whites are typically hyper-critical of black actions.[4]

Thus, when considering how poverty or lack of access to adequate resources is a common, connecting narrative for so many black and brown bodies struggling for survival within the throes of Inner City, USA, is it any surprise that the ability or perceived ability to overcome these circumstances would also be celebrated? A simple trip to your local book store will reveal many a magazine cover that references monetary gain or lifestyles associated with significant economic gain (e.g., "Robb Report," "Car and Driver" or the fact that the average issue of "Home & Garden" magazine does not feature residences located in low income areas) — quite logical given the repeated, imputed emphasis on economic prosperity within the American capitalistic economy.[5] Game show contestants and lottery winners are hardly shamed for emoting over their newfound fortunes, often "earned" through the gauntlet of chance and circumstance. The celebration of money and its trappings is not problematic. Provided the vestiges of negrophobia still linger, the imagery associated with urban black males performing the celebrating apparently is problematic.

Many black males are thus frequently criticized by the mainstream as having a warped view of money and its appropriate use.[6] Spending hundreds of dollars on a gold chain is an obvious waste of resources, yet, spending thousands of dollars on a ice-carved statute that spouts vodka out of its fountain is a worthy investment for the corporate Holiday party.[7] In other words, both can be categorized as superfluous or as necessary depending upon "perspective." For, just as — at least for those in attendance — an argument can be made that the opportunity to link together as a unit and collectively display appreciation for prior hard work and achievement, thereby justifying the expense on the ice carving at the Holiday party, perhaps much of the same can be said about the gold chain. Perhaps the only difference being that instead of investing in a memory that tangibly lasts for one evening, the gold chain can be worn multiple evenings (or days).

It is important to interrogate the true motiviation of such criticism, for a mere thirty minutes in front of any television in America in the month of December will expose one to plenty of advertisements for jewelry, as "there is no better way to say 'I love you'" during the holiday season than with diamonds, for instance. Jewelry unto itself, is not the problem. And as illustrated within the foregoing paragraph, many a corporate actor routinely makes lavish expenditures without similar scrutiny or criticism. In rare instances do such purchases come to light, and only when the subject of a scandal.[8] Hence, mainstream media criticisms aside, our concern is how do the actual practicioners of Hip Hop view money? Within the Hip Hop multi-verse, while not all references to income are holy and pure, here money is largely a tool with a dual purpose: 1) to literally purchase one's "freedom" from the throes of the Unholy Trinity and all the indignities and inconveninces that inadequate resources can impose upon an individual and 2) to illustrate one's "value" in society. The stubborn persistence of the Unholy Trinity suggests numerous obstacles and a large amount of negative social inertia that must be overcome. Making it "out of the ghetto" and bypassing middle and upper middle class status for the rarc and privileged air of the upper class by simply "studying hard" in school or by "pulling oneself up by their bootstraps (even if they do not have bootstraps)" is virtually akin to say, winning the lottery! Thus, any economic success is "proof" that the individual did "something right" and is rightfully celebrated.

However, of the three prongs within the American Dream Triple Team, arguably Hip Hop's relationship with Sex has been most controversial. It is unsurprising that expressions of sexuality by urban black youth have been demonized and criticized roundly by mainstream media. Blacks have been associated with higher instances of sexual deviance generally.[9] Misogyny is the degradation of the female image based upon a presumed power dynamic of male superiority. Misogyny is damaging to all humans and not just women. And yes, misogyny is found within Hip Hop. Misogyny is found within most of mainstream American culture as well, but black bodies have been the traditional battleground regarding such action.[10] Most examples of misogyny are improperly assigned to Hip Hop when they should be assigned to Rap Music — for, that is what sells. Examples of misogyny within Hip Hop do exist, however, and we shall not exonerate but merely explicate the context for such examples.

While some references to sex within Rap Music are downright pornographic, within Hip Hop, this is not always the case. So many

Americans are fixated on the pleasurable acquisition of sex, money and power, practicioners of Hip Hop being no exception. Yet, in the sense that Hip Hop disciples use the genre as a tool to proclaim and reclaim their humanity, dignity and respect, an aspect of the human existence is fantasy. Impoverished, marginalized black and brown people are allowed to have fantasies too. Sexual ones even.

# YOU'RE WELCOME

In the ten examples that follow, consider the Unholy Trinity and how it may inform or influence the track profiled. Representative examples of the Aspiration HipHopetype include, but are not limited to:

| CLASSIC Aspiration Example #1 | | | |
|---|---|---|---|
| **Artist** | **Track** | **Sample** | **When** |
| Biggie Smalls | "Juicy" (1994) | "The Moët and Alizé keep me pissy; girls they used to diss me, now they write letters cause they miss me. I never thought it could happen -- this rappin' stuff; I was too used to packing gats and stuff. " | 1:41 mark |
| **LINK:** https://www.youtube.com/watch?v=4M0ObL56C0A | | | |

**Brief Analysis:** When Biggie raps about women in his life, at least in this track, it is not for the purposes of hedonistic titilation. While we do see such examples within Rap Music as well as within larger American society (think Hollywood), Biggie's aim is different here. Biggie uses women as a metric with which to measure his increased social attractability and "value" within society. Despite suffering from Rejection, Biggie aspired for more in life and somehow found his entrée to the American Dream through his craft of rapping, which in turn made him more desirable. Biggie's humanity is validated as he has come "full circle" from an anti-Horatio Alger life of Rejection, poverty and crime. **PACKING GATS** refers to Biggie carrying firearms as part and parcel of an illegal street life.

| Aspiration Example #2 | | | |
|---|---|---|---|
| **Artist** | **Track** | **Sample** | **When** |
| T3 | "Count the Ways" (2004) by Slum Village feat. Dwele, Elzhi & T3 | "We roll out then we shift to step three, hotel accomodation is lovely; there's no way they hand us the wrong key, top floor you know the penthouse suite..." | 1:13 mark |
| **LINK:** https://www.youtube.com/watch?v=6lTdcjlwGBQ | | | |

**Brief Analysis:** Here, this fantasy track revolves around sexual fantasy. Elzhi and T3 team up to paint an ideal picture of how exactly they would romance their potential paramour if provided the opportunity. It is unclear from the track whether the authors position themselves as actually having the ability (financially) to do so, however, they are at least half way there in having envisioned the ideal scenario in the first place.

Lastly, even though the track explicitly describes a sexual fantasy, this track is not representative of a sexually explicit fantasy. In describing the various "steps" leading up to potential consummation of the imagined ideal relationship, it is quite evident that knitting a scarf together is not the end goal of the various steps described. Yet, the verbal intercourse before the presumed "ultimate act" is just as important as the act itself. In other words, the elaborate fantasy description — even if not real — is nonetheless real evidence that the authors are thinking about more than just sex. The authors are clearly in tune with the entire mood and orientation of their partner's needs, and more tellingly, the authors' fantasy was framed around fulfilling their partner's fantasy.

## Aspiration Example #3

**CLASSIC**

| Artist | Track | Sample | When |
|---|---|---|---|
| Public Enemy | "Fight the Power" (1990) | "We got to fight the powers that be!" | 0:47 mark |
| **LINK:** https://www.youtube.com/watch?v=8PaoLy7PHwk | | | |

**Brief Analysis:** In referencing power, literally, Chuck D of Public Enemy outlines his ideal vision of what society would look like if more members of the community would purposely resist the mainstream status quo.

## Aspiration Example #4

| Artist | Track | Sample | When |
|---|---|---|---|
| Ice T | "Girls L.G.B.N.A.F." (1988) | "Tonight I'm trying to make this real clear, dear; I've no time to whisper in your ear." | 0:36 mark |
| **LINK:** https://www.youtube.com/watch?v=5MX1leC30b0 | | | |

**Brief Analysis:** Moral merits aside, the idea that anyone would be as so bold and brass to create a song with an acronym that stands for "Girls Let's Get Butt Naked and F*ck" is actually quite original and remarkable. It is exceedingly blunt and therefore violates most rules of social convention. Yet, this is exactly what Hip Hop does — it interrupts our traditional mainstream messaging and challenges us to think critically. Now, after considering Ice T's methodology of communication, it is up to the listener to either give kudos or criticism over Ice T's style, but at the very least, he has the listener thinking. Is Ice T being crass and promoting a poor model of male to female communication? Or, is Ice T liberating himself from the pseudo social mores that litter our linguistic landscape and is simply mowing through to the bottom line — a bottom line reached every day during the day in majority white populated soap operas where monogamy is dysfunctional and infrequent fornication is exceptional. As of time of print, Ice T is still married to a model named Coco, had his own reality TV show and a starring role within a mainstream crime show entitled "Law & Order: Special Victims Unit" as possible proof that he was not socially ostracized or punished for getting to the point. If anything, perhaps we can say the opposite....

## Aspiration Example #5

| Artist | Track | Sample | When |
|--------|-------|--------|------|
| Mack 10 | "I Want It All" (1999)<br><br>by Warren G feat. Mack 10 | "From net workin' and hustlin' no doubt I got clout; and live the lifestyle that Robin Leach talk about." | 1:54 mark |
| **LINK:** https://www.youtube.com/watch?v=3YG8gV3UDyE | | | |

**Brief Analysis:** In referencing mostly money and power, Warren G and Mack 10 inform the listener that they are very goal-oriented. While Rap Music is rightfully criticized for its fetishization of material culture, within this track the listener can discern the humanity behind such acquisitions. The track is very Aspirational as the listener is told what the author desires as evidence of their triumph over the Unholy Trinity and their general success in life.

## Aspiration Example #6

| Artist | Track | Sample | When |
|--------|-------|--------|------|
| Ed O. G. | "Be a Father" (1991)<br><br>by Ed O. G. & Da Bulldogs | "See I hate when a brother makes a child and denies it; thinking that money is the answer so he buys it — a whold bunch of gifts and a lot of presents; but it's not the presents, its your presence and your essence of being there and showing the baby that you care." | 1:14 mark |
| **LINK:** https://www.youtube.com/watch?v=ZQMVsQW_kjM | | | |

**Brief Analysis:** This track is aspirational for a larger community of black males specifically. As a result of the Unholy Trinity, many black males are separated or compromised within their families. During the Era of Enslavement, when white slave owners would separate a black slave father from his family, it was "good business." Currently, when black fathers separate from their families, it is bad business. Further, according to socially influential public documents such as the "Moniyhan Report,"[II] black males are freely blamed wiithout contextualizing their struggles within a historical, systematic struggle. By no means is this a space to exonerate or excuse dead beat dads as they rightfully should feel shamed. Equally as shameful are the circumstances challenging the long-term viability of black families within urban environments. Ed O G is using moral suasion as a technique to encourage others to strive for their best and to motivate others to avoid such socially destructive results despite the challenges. A track like this reminds listeners of the chasm between Rap Music and Hip Hop, for as much as society says it prefers "socially responsible" messaging, this song will never see the light of airplay since it likely would not be deemed "hype enough" to play on the radio.

| Aspiration Example #7 | | | |
|---|---|---|---|
| **Artist** | **Track** | **Sample** | **When** |
| Rick Ross | "Magnificent" (2009)<br><br>by Rick Ross feat. John Legend | "I"m a don, I'm a boss, I'm a prof, I'm a "G" -- I'm a CEO which means that I profit off of me." | 1:05 mark |
| **LINK:** https://www.youtube.com/watch?v=XIWEbmQt8EQ | | | |
| **BONUS:** https://www.youtube.com/watch?v=n77E2OsrwW8 (Rejection) | | | |

**Brief Analysis:** Sir Ross teams up with Grammy-Award winning tenor John Legend to paint a magnificent picture of what life is like based upon personal individual success. Horatio Alger would be quite fond of this track indeed. The American Dream Triple Team is all highlighted here — just within the chorus alone! If the reader is still unclear, Sir Ross's video will clear any misconceptions as to how or why this is an Aspirational track. Questions can be fairly posed about whether Sir Ross **ACTUALLY** lives the lifestyle portrayed and depicted within the video, but similar to Slum Village in "Count the Ways," his actual material is immaterial. The image in fact now exists. See the **BONUS** link for additional Aspirational context (due to Rejection) when Ross recalls in an interview being the "fat black kid with poor shoes" when younger. When "afforded" the opportunity, he challenges and changes this painfully impoverished narrative.

| Aspiration Example #8 | | | |
|---|---|---|---|
| **Artist** | **Track** | **Sample** | **When** |
| All Natural | "It's OK" (1998) | "It's OK, you ain't got to play the role of the fool; it's OK, you can be dope and still finish school." | 1:44 mark |
| LINK: https://www.youtube.com/watch?v=BCPUkVHMsV8&list=PLk8KAfSHjIu5wANvjjt2mgTkGuKZINLt2 | | | |

**Brief Analysis:** All Natural comprises a duo of underground MCs who hail from Chicago. Unlike Rick Ross, very few within mainstream circles have likely heard of their album. Perhaps if more did, we all would be better served for similar to Ed O G's "Be a Father to Your Child," All Natural's aspirational "want" is communal, rather than individualized, narcissitic or solipsistic in nature. This track is aspirational in that it liberates young men from having to over compensate for their struggles with the Unholy Trinity and allows for them to be OK with who they are — regardless of how much access to sex, money and power that they have.

| Aspiration Example #9 | | | |
|---|---|---|---|
| **Artist** | **Track** | **Sample** | **When** |
| Bun B | "Candy" (2006) by Little Brother feat. Bun B and Darien Brockington | "If I ain't got nuthin' new I ain't coming outside; that goes for clothes, rolls, shoes, jewels and rides." | 0:50 mark |
| LINK: https://www.youtube.com/watch?v=IVoJlD5X7Wk | | | |

**Brief Analysis:** In this upbeat, light-hearted track, Bun B articulates his ideal vision as to how he wants others to see him **IN PUBLIC**. He validates his own existence within society and on the planet in contrast to how he might be perceived if his image identity was left up to the Unholy Trinity.

## CLASSIC Aspiration Example #10

| Artist | Track | Sample | When |
|---|---|---|---|
| Kool G. Rap<br><br>Kool G. Rap<br>(feat. Nas) | "Fast Life" (1995) | "Champagne wishes and caviar dreams a team that's getting cream; with sales of fish scales from triple beams, I gleam..." | 0:38 mark |
| **LINK:** https://www.youtube.com/watch?v=zp5EOREHcuY | | | |

**Brief Analysis:** Kool G Rap and Nas use very vivid descriptions in a masterful style to paint a picture for the listener. The rather smooth and **COOL** "Happy" beat sampled from the eighties R&B group Surface in the background belies how complex the rhyme scheme is as every line from both artists is literally chock full of syllables. And perhaps that is the point: they take the complex and make it appear simple as if their accomplishments were all accomplished with "no sweat." To this last point, if you have not seen the video, you will only come to understand the track's "Classic" designation after seeing the treadmill!

# BEFORE YOU BOUNCE

- The **Aspiration HipHopetype** speaks to the desire for better in life

- **FEATURES:** improvement, personal & collective

- **YOUR TURN:** Is it any marvel or wonder that those of a marginalized class, likely surrounded by people who look nothing like the glamorized depictions of beauty onscreen from whence they were little, would not also take the opportunity to flex their social muscles and (perhaps ill-advisedly) attempt to display their value and worth through their "accepted presence" around similar type of women? If you were to film a video tomorrow, would you prefer "Hollywood babes" or "around the way girls"? How would your overall message be altered by the mere skin color of these included women?

# 8

# RECOGNITION

## HipHopetype #6

| Rejection | Description | Demonstration | Prescription | Aspiration | Recognition |
|---|---|---|---|---|---|
| HipHopetypes Corresponding with Honored Hip Hop Elements | | | | | |
| MC | DJ | Graffiti | Knowledge of Self | B-boy/girl | ALL |
| Unholy Trinity Antidote to the Corresponding Anti-Creative Forces | | | | | |
| FEAR | | | FASCINATION | | |
| exclusion | delusion | marginalization | indecision | desolation | invalidation |
| HipHopetypes Ethos as Evidence of Creative GENIUS | | | | | |
| FAITH | | | FACILITATION | | |
| inclusion | clarity | empowerment | wisdom | optimism | dignity & respect |

# THE OLD TRICKS KEEP COMING

This HipHopetype encapsulates internal recognition of the difficulty and **GENIUS** that many within the mainstream may take for granted on a daily basis. In realizing the complexity and beauty that the harmony of Hip Hop has to offer to help cope with the effects of the Unholy Trinity, it is not uncommon for grateful Hip Hop practioners who have respect for the genre and what it has done for them personally and professionally to actively incorporate the medium as a legitimate and effective bridge to their interdisciplinary works. In turn, these supportive Hip Hop practioners encourage education by their listening audience of older songs and artists within Hip Hop that should always remain held in high esteem.

While the first HipHopetype analyzed was Rejection, we now have come full circle to one of the highest honors one can receive, which is voluntary, unforced and sincere Recognition by one's peers. Recognition is the ultimate acknowledgement of dignity and respect.

# RECOGNIZE FOOL!

Many of Hip Hop's dedicated practioners still are smarting from the idea that Hip Hop and by virtue its creators are not worthy of dignity or respect. Unlike classical music, which is lauded by scholars and laymen alike as having intellectual properties and the mere listening to it will improve brain function,[1] Hip Hop was first met with an anti-intellectualist critique. Now, a large swath of Hip Hop has been pawned off as pop culture — Rap Music can be seen and heard within mainstream culture and it retains an almost ubiquitous presence in contemporary slang as well as mainstream corporate advertisements, and Top 40 playlists. When Hip Hop first came on the scene, many critics reviled Hip Hop as not having any long-standing staying power.[2] Many critics incorrectly predicted Hip Hop as being a fad that only would appeal to a small section of society.

Thus, as a clever attempt to build itself up, Hip Hop artists have been discriminating against that which they deem to be real Hip Hop versus everything else. Hip Hop artists recognize Hip Hop as more than just music, but rather treat it as a culture, a mindset, a way of life, an ethos. Hip Hop artists are very grateful for the outlet Hip Hop has provided to express oneself, explore new ideas and feel free. Hip Hop has restored humanity, dignity and respect for many of its listeners and performers as an antidote to the Unholy Trinity. Just like a proud alumnus may make mention of the institution from whence they graduated, the same is true for Hip Hop, those who have made it out or are making their way through are very much protective.

Within this HipHopetype, it is therefore not uncommon to hear the author make explicit and direct reference to the instution of Hip Hop itself **AND WILL MENTION HIP HOP BY NAME**. Additionally, it is not uncommon to hear dedicated artists frequently insert "complaints" in their rhymes about individuals who do not respect the craft (i.e., **F.A.K.E. M.C.s**) of Hip Hop or about the larger industry itself and the trend towards commercialization of an ideal that has no true price.

# TIME TO SHOUT OUT THE SHOUT OUT

Why is the shout out so important?

Again, when wrestling with the throes of the Unholy Trinity, one can feel downright invalidated. Recognition is an aspect of humanity.

In deference and homage to an art form that has allowed many a person to earn a prosperous living that they may not otherwise earn doing other things, artists shout out Hip Hop itself. Secondly, to break free of oppression is significant. When people do so, no matter how much money they have, they are often "indebted" to those who helped them intellectually, socially or materially prosper.

Shout outs can take place at any point in time, whether they be at the beginning, worked into the middle, or in a string of names listed at the end of a track. Frequently, the performing artist will recognize other (Hip Hop) artists that influenced them (to do Hip Hop). Recognition is not necessarily reserved only for "name brand" rap artists — it can apply to any soul who helped sustain belief and confidence in the Vocalist — especially before the Vocalist became a Vocalist. As non-artists may be recognized (e.g., mom, dad, friend, DJ), it is usually within the context of recognizing this individual's influence in helping the author breaking free of the Unholy Trinity, which ultimately is still "political" in tone. Consider how Talib Kweli wrote entire songs about Lauryn Hill and G.U.R.U. while Common composed one for Assata Shakur and Skyzoo did director Spike Lee.[3]

If "imitation is the highest form of flattery," then whenever an artist imitates or duplicates lyrics or style of another Hip Hop artist, this act also qualifies as a shout out. Snoop Dogg's "Who Got Some Gangsta Sh*t" starts off nearly exactly the same as Ice T's "6 N the Morning" track. Artists like Fabolous and Jadakiss recorded their version of the Nas and AZ classic "Life's a B*tch," complete with similar rhyme schemes and the same beat. In keeping with Chuck D's axiom that Hip Hop functions as a "Black CNN," practioners use the channels available to them to communicate the people and pioneers that are important to them. Shout outs are another, original, creative way of saying "Hi Mom!" Appropriate, seeing how Hip Hop has given birth to many a new perspective, source of income or way of life for many who could only see clouds during sunny days. To this end, Common created a shout out tradition whereby when alive, his father, Lonnie Lynn had the "last word" on the last track on every one of Common's albums with a positive, poetic commentary over a jazzy instrumental.[4]

# PAY DUES

Respect is not purchased; it is earned. For those who labor and are serious about their craft, the results will be self evident. There are a myriad of ways to earn "props." Record sales are demonstrative, but not dispositive of success within the Hip Hop industry. For instance, to return to the scene of the crime, Iggy Azalea has significant record sales, Grammy award wins, NBA husband and all the positive press and trappings of a bonafide Hip Hop star. Everything, except the respect of true Hip Hop fans.[5]

The bottom line is that Hip Hop practioners are very critical of those who fail to see Hip Hop's true purpose and threaten to diminish its value. To repeat, Hip Hop is one of the few "industries" or public arenas whereby: 1) black males are largely in control, 2) black males are portrayed as powerful and 3) black males freely exhibit behaviors of freedom itself. A profound indebtedness is cultivated for the source of this freedom. While the American Dream Triple Team of sex, money and power are always contemplated, Hip Hop has also allowed for intellectual, emotional and spiritual freedom of black males to express themselves as a rather public/private form of therapeutic self-care in order to maintain mental health. In other words, Hip Hop, has "paid dues" for many practioners and has proven itself loyal, faithful and true. When one is clear on identifying the source that sustains their own life, they are likely to dedicate their life back.

# YOU'RE WELCOME

In the ten examples that follow, consider the Unholy Trinity and how it may inform or influence the track profiled. Representative examples of the Rejection HipHopetype include, but are not limited to:

| *CLASSIC* Recognition Example #1 | | | |
|---|---|---|---|
| **Artist** | **Track** | **Sample** | **When** |
| Biggie Smalls | "Juicy" (1994) | "Peace to Ron G, Brucey B, Kid Capri; Funkmaster Flex, Lovebug Starski. I'm blowing up like you thought I would; call the crib, same number, same hood — it's all good." | 0:57 mark |
| **LINK:** https://www.youtube.com/watch?v=4M0ObL56C0A | | | |

**Brief Analysis:** The first stanza of Biggie's Hip Hop classic reads more like an introduction to a history of Hip Hop text. Before he regales the listener with the Aspiration an Demonstration HipHopetypes having personally triumphed over forces of the Unholy Trinity as alluded to within the introduction (e.g., "This is dedicated to the teachers who told me I'd never amount to nuthin'") he informs the listener of his artistic lineage. Biggie is very clear about his place within Hip Hop lore. Biggie is deliberate in recognizing the pioneers of Hip Hop that paved the way for his platform today. "It was all a dream! I used to read 'Word Up' magazine, Salt n Pepa, Heavy D up in the limousine." Biggie's homage to history starts with one of the first magazines dedicated to the genre of Hip Hop and Hip Hop news (which was rare) and gives a "shout out" to early influential Hip Hop acts Salt n Pepa (which was an innovative female trio) and Heavy D — a fair complexioned African American male from Detroit who was known for his energetic dance moves despite appearing to be "overweight" for his height. "I used to hang the posters on my wall. Mister Magic Rap Attack, Marley Marl; I used to listen until my tape popped, smoking on bamboo, sipping on private stock. Remember Rapping Duke? Da ha, da ha! I never thought that Hip Hop would take it this far." Biggie's reference to his "tape popped" is also a shout out to the early days when brothers would try to "share" their music on the go by walking around with what was called a "boom box" as opposed to the individualized earphone culture that is currently popular. The large radios played cassette tapes before music was placed on CDs or housed within electronic files. Rapping Duke was an early rapper who stylized himself as John Wayne. It was corny. It was also a crossover hit. Later in the track Biggie says "peace to Brucie B..." — this is also a form of recognition as he is recognizing people in the neighborhood or people within his life that he respects or is indebted to based upon the love they gave him when he had nothing but the Unholy Trinity to dog him.

| RECOGNITION Example #2 | | | |
|---|---|---|---|
| **Artist** | **Track** | **Sample** | **When** |
| Fabolous | "Sacrifices" (2013) | "When you go, you're just gone, all we missing is payments; Dr. King fought for my freedom that I risked just to pay rent." | 1:37 mark |
| LINK: https://www.youtube.com/watch?v=sOfFyHQPJu0 | | | |

**Brief Analysis:** The rapper Fabolous recorded the song "Sacrifices" in 2013. Yet, he consistently makes reference to figures from the past that he wishes to recognize as influential upon his present narrative. In addition to recognizing his grandmother for trying to keep him alive through feeding ("she just handing me sandwiches"), Fabolous dips all the way back into the Civil Rights Era to recognize both Dr. Martin Luther King and Rosa Parks ("Rosa Parks took that charge for you, that's a sacrifice"). If you think about it, it is not often that a contemporary song will reference historical figures by name. In so doing, Fabolous recognizes his relationship with history and the continued influence of the Unholy Trinity by stating that Rosa Parks and Dr. Martin Luther King made sacrifices for all Americans to enjoy the rights they presently enjoy.

## RECOGNITION Example #3

| Artist | Track | Sample | When |
|--------|-------|--------|------|
| 2Pac (Tupac Shakur) | "Representin' 93" (1993) | "Peace to Redman, Treach, Vin Rock, Kay Gee the great one..." | entire Verse 2 starting at the 1:33 mark |

LINK: https://www.youtube.com/watch?v=9kLYYOtrdU0

**Brief Analysis:** The late great Tupac Shakur in his "Strictly Representin'" track provides yet another installment of a growing litany of songs that take significant recording time to recognize or provide public "shout outs" to early pioneers or influential Hip Hop artists who paved the way (e.g., as Positive K once famously said, "What more can I say? I wouldn't be here today if the old school didn't pave the way"). This is unique to the genre of Hip Hop. We must think carefully about other genres of music where it is considered fashionable for a contemporary artist to spend an entire song listing off the names of prior artists they admire or wish to thank or whom they found influential. Here, Hip Hop evidences its communal-based orientation and philosophy. Tupac also smugly demonstrates to the listener that he is connected to the pulse entitled Hip Hop when he rattles off well-know, established, famous names and simply packages them as "just a coupla motherf*ckas that I know."

## CLASSIC RECOGNITION Example #4

| Artist | Track | Sample | When |
|--------|-------|--------|------|
| Common Sense  **NOTE**: the Chicago artist Common was known as *Common Sense* at the time | "I Used to Love H.E.R." (1994) | "Slim was fresh yo, when she was underground; original, pure, untampered, a down sister — boy I tell ya, I miss her." | 1:02 mark |

LINK: https://www.youtube.com/watch?v=fMnExsbhgPI

**BONUS:** The Roots, ft. Common, "Act Too (Love of My Life)" https://www.youtube.com/watch?v=tjIcga4Afrg

**Brief Analysis:** This ground-breaking track "shouts out" Hip Hop itself, being one of the first and arguably most well-known innovative tracks that personified Hip Hop in the form of a person with whom Common had a relationship. Many have since adopted this formula and have continued with this metaphor to express reservations about where Hip Hop is going as a culture relative to "her" potential and promise as a once fair maiden.

## CLASSIC RECOGNITION Example #5

| Artist | Track | Sample | When |
|---|---|---|---|
| Nas | "The World is Yours" (1994) | "To everybody in Queens, the foundaion, the world is yours; to everybody uptown, yo, the world is yours, the world is yours..." | 4:07 mark |
| LINK: https://www.youtube.com/watch?v=_srvHOu75vM | | | |

**Brief Analysis:** One of the more famous examples, helping to formalize a technique wherein at the conclusion of a track, the artist "recognizes" certain special individuals from significant locations in his life.

## RECOGNITION Example #6

| Artist | Track | Sample | When |
|---|---|---|---|
| G.U.R.U. | "Soliloquoy of Chaos" (1992) by Gangstarr | "Five carloads deep, time to go to a show; got massive crew and we're ready to roll so..." | 0:29 mark |
| LINK: https://www.youtube.com/watch?v=45QOPG_XkOM | | | |

**Brief Analysis:** Before you is a very clever example where Guru sets the stage for a party that had a mishap, but in the process, shouts out by name virtually everyone in his "five carloads deep" crew (as in, at least thirty different individuals!). Knowing this list was not exhaustive, he is smooth enough to state at the end of his string that "and to the rest of the crew, you know the bond is strong; and you know who's who, so let me not prolong" before transitioning into his descriptive and prescriptive story.

## RECOGNITION Example #7

| Artist | Track | Sample | When |
|---|---|---|---|
| Da Youngsta's | "Hip Hop Ride (Mellow Mix)" (1994) | "Peace to Shanté, Sweet Tee and Sah-B -- representing Hip Hop lovely." | 2:05 mark |
| LINK: https://www.youtube.com/watch?v=WOUVkcLw8uM | | | |

**Brief Analysis:** This is an explicit shout out to Hip Hop itself. Three verses, with one dedicated to female Hip Hop pioneers show that unlike other musical genres, there is this heightened sense of self-awareness within Hip Hop itself.

## RECOGNITION Example #8

| Artist | Track | Sample | When |
|---|---|---|---|
| J. Cole | "Fire Squad" (2014) | "This year I'll prolly go to the awards dappered down; Watch Iggy win a Grammy as I try to crack a smile I'm just playin', but all good jokes contain true shit; Same rope you climb up on, they'll hang you with ." | 3:24 mark |
| LINK: https://www.youtube.com/watch?v=-MGB_G_ZjMo | | | |

**Brief Analysis:** J. Cole makes mention and recognition of one of the more pressing political issues facing Hip Hop as a larger subculture and community; namely, the tension present between appreciation and appropriation of Hip Hop by mainstream (read white) America. "History repeats itself and that's just how it goes/Same way that these rappers always bite each others flows/Same thing that my n*gga Elvis did with Rock n' Roll/Justin Timberlake, Eminem, and then Macklemore." We explore this topic in greater detail in Chapter 9, "Appreciation/Appropriation."

| RECOGNITION Example #9 | | | |
|---|---|---|---|
| **Artist** | **Track** | **Sample** | **When** |
| AZ | "Fan Mail" (2002) | "Peace Allah, hope this scribe reach your hands in good health; as for self, no sense of worrying, my cards been dealt" | 0:21 mark |
| **LINK:** https://www.youtube.com/watch?v=26AucRfmnL8 | | | |

**Brief Analysis:** AZ does two things with this track, make that three. First, he cleverly composes a song where the premise is that he is reading two letters composed to him, presumably by fans of his music. Yet, these letters are quite revealing. More than mere attempts to offer adulation for a celebrity figure, these letters (one by a male and one by a female) offer sincere insight into the power of sincere communication. AZ unwittingly touches upon a commentary that perhaps many of older generations bemoan as true; that in spite of our electronic, instantaneous interconnectedness through the internet and modern social media, that us members of society are still ineffective in communicating honest, substantive thoughts. After all, one can only do so much with video snippets of ten seconds or less or with typed messages limited to 140 characters or less. Enter the age-old, ancient craft of letter writing! The time required to compose one's thoughts evidence the more thoughtful nature of the message. The listener knows that what flows from AZ lips is important — even if coming from "unimportant" members of society.

Second, AZ recognizes the people of his community that are struggling against the forces of the Unholy Trinity, particularly the first verse where he gives a stylized and extended shout out to prison culture. Through the fan's "letter," AZ takes the time to describe the generic experience of how those who are locked up often lament about how they are often "locked away" and forgotten, making positive re-entry into society more difficult.

Thirdly, AZ locates himself at the center of praise by "real people" from the hood, which thereby only reaffirms his authenticity and value to true underground Hip Hop. While *you* may not have heard of him (e.g., on the radio), real people with real problems have. And they appreciate him.

| RECOGNITION Example #10 | | | |
| --- | --- | --- | --- |
| **Artist** | **Track** | **Sample** | **When** |
| Mr. Funke AKA Chief Rocka | "Tic Toc (DJ Duke remix)" (1994)<br><br>by Lords of The Underground | "I remember way back in the days on my block when the kids used to meet up in the hallway and rock; on Martin Luther King Boulevard with P.C., Wise, Easy Ed and my brother Hard Bernard." | 2:56 mark |
| **LINK:** https://www.youtube.com/watch?v=4O11zBhKmzw | | | |

**Brief Analysis:** The Chief Rocka takes us down memory lane, all the way to Martin Luther King Boulevard. After MLK's assassination in the 1968, many cities began honoring and recognizing his impact by renaming streets or high schools after him. Can you guess which part of town? MLK Blvd is a euphemistic clue that Chief Rocka came from a gritty part of Jersey. Yet, he is humble and appreciative of the life lessons he learned. He concludes clearly and convincingly: "No matter how large I get the fire still burns; from the hood I came and to the hood I must return."

---

# BEFORE YOU BOUNCE

- The **Recognition HipHopetype** speaks to dignity and respect

- **FEATURES:** "shout outs" to those within Hip Hop or Hip Hop itself

- **BONUS:** "The Definition," DJ Jazzy Jeff (feat. Kel Spencer); https://www.youtube.com/watch?v=hpU6pUaGdII

# 9

# APPRECIATION/
# APPROPRIATION

## White Noise

# THE PICKS KEEP COMING

Let's "take it to the streets" and hear appropriation as explained by the urban philosopher Delondo Nugent: **"White boys rock Snoop Doggy Dogg just as hard as me — but I'm the n*gga!"**[1] While exceedingly succinct, Mr. Nugent's larger point is that based upon overarching principles of negrophobia, whenever blacks commit expressive acts, they are typically criticized, but similar white actions are not nearly as scrutinized.[2] What this means for Hip Hop is that what was once bemoaned as antithetical to America when it had a distinctly black aesthetic is now mainstream America once filtered through the lens and imagery of whiteness.

The appropriation concept undoubtedly is confusing for many since it appears to display "sensitivity" over those within the Hip Hop community "not sharing" their craft. In actuality, the senstitivity comes not from outsiders appreciating Hip Hop, but rather from an outsider exploiting Hip Hop for one's personal benefit without any true appreciation at all. A question to ask is whether the opposite is true, rather, whether blacks or Latinos have the ability to take aspects of "white culture" and sell it to whites (e.g., classical or country music). This driving force behind this question is one of negotiated power and typically operates upon a one-way street.

Appreciation or appropriation? That is the question! Appreciation is unconditional. A sincere appreciation means that one can enjoy the craft without any expectation of a return. Appropriation is conditional. Typically, appropriation is performed with an expectation of a return — whether it be additional attention or revenue. Now that Hip Hop has grown into a multi-billion dollar genre of global proportion[3] its audience has naturally diversified. Once the original province of mostly black and brown individuals fighting against the anti-Horatio forces of the Unholy Trinity, Hip Hop has now taken on a universal meaning worldwide. Many people from many races from many different places across the world interpret and re-interpret Hip Hop through their struggles for humanity, on whatever plane of existence in which they find themselves.

If one goes to Germany, France, Egypt or South Africa, they will find local rappers flowing in their native tongues. Thus, not everyone who currently composes a Hip Hop track will necessarily describe and address life as seen from the nitty gritty streets of "Inner City, USA." Hip Hop and its complex aesthetics and expressions now constitute the foundation of a larger culture, loosely organized and cultivated around the elements and corresponding HipHopetypes. Moreover, Hip Hop is by design an inclusive culture and open to all.

Including white Americans.

Herein lies our dilemma for this chapter.

What we will parse out here is the difference between appreciation versus appropriation. As stated earlier, more white Americans patronize and support Hip Hop now than when it first arrived on scene — in fact, most of the (formal) consumers are white.[4] So then, what does this mean for our "post-racial society?"[5] Is this cultural amalgamation proof of our progress that we now lay claim to a day where people will no longer be judged by the color of their skin, but by the content of their character? Or, is something else going on?

For starters, there is nothing problematic with whites embracing and appreciating Hip Hop. But there is something problematic with whites exploiting and appropriating Hip Hop.

# WHAT'S WITH THE ATTITUDE?

Appropriation is sensitive topic within many black and brown circles as it is an age-old topic. Whether it be Aunt Jemima's Pancake Syrup or jazz "ambassadors" used during the war effort[6] to savvy marketers who employ "street lingo" to better sell their products, history is replete with examples of whites openly using blacks and black culture to materially benefit themselves. It must be said that Hip Hop is merely the most recent gift of "black music." Starting with the negro spirituals that were "shared" and adopted by whites during the Era of Enslavement, blacks also provided the innovative and original sound of jazz after the turn of the century. When jazz music first arrived, it too, was roundly criticized before being internalized decades later.[7] The same goes for blues music, rock n' roll and R&B.

Perhaps nowhere do we see appropriation best except in the world of corporate marketing. The result is that many people end up confused as to what is true Hip Hop since highly visible corporations utilizing Hip Hop have significant exposure and distribution channels that challenge widespread underground dissemination. Thus, the "real Hip Hop" remains in the background while distorted images of Rap Music become synonymous with mainstream culture. The cycle feeds upon itself and Hip Hop gets blamed for any deleterious effects while individuals or entities outside of Hip Hop reap the profits.

Appropriation requires three parts: 1) **an agent**, or individual or entity that is leveraging the cultural artifact in question 2) **an artifact**, or tangible, symbolic representation of a culture external to the agent and 3) **an approach**, or methodology of publicly leveraging the external culture, whether it be through a humorous commercial or a half-serious attempt to demonstrate competency for personal profit.

In returning to Mr. Nugent's opening, whites routinely criticize blacks for having "attitude" privately, but then turn around and exploit this same "attitude" publicly for profit. For example, consider this "in your face" photograph of a public service announcement advertised by the Ad Council on behalf of the U.S. Department of Agriculture, Forestry Division. The finger point is reminiscent of rap culture that commands attention with stylistic poses on album covers. The ad's non-conventional phrasing comes directly from Hip Hop parlance; instead of saying "You really should consider going to get

Photo taken by author of empaneled ad at Metro bus stop @ intersection of Connecticut Avenue and Military Rd, in the Northwest section of Washington, D.C. @ Spring, 2013.

some exercise today," the **GENIUS** of Hip Hop slanguage and thought economy simply states: "Get your exercise on." So, perhaps the clever joke is that instead of getting one's "smoke" on, the U.S. government wants you to get your "Smokey" on instead. How clever indeed.

To review, what is now happening to Hip Hop also happened to jazz, rock n' roll, disco and R&B. The people who started real Hip Hop were not white, blond and from Australia — and they darn sure were not winning Grammys and getting paid for boasting about how "Fancy" they were for drinking liquor with no chaser. But rather, Hip Hop's originators offered cogent and concise articulated critiques about social, economic and political failings of which they truly cared.

# NO THANK YOU

What follows are ten examples of Appropriation that illustrate how mostly white entities have taken aspects of black culture for personal benefit, with virtually none of the profits being shared with the actual agents of the culture. Again, Hip Hop is created for the world to share, not shame. In the examples that follow, consider the Unholy Trinity and how it may inform or influence the scenario. Representative examples of Appropriation include, but are not limited to:

| APPROPRIATION Example #1 | | |
|---|---|---|
| **Agent** | **Artifact** | **Approach** |
| *Vogue* Magazine | black "booty" or "back" | Feature article detailing/declaring "new trend." |
| **LINK:** http://www.vogue.com/1342927/booty-in-pop-culture-jennifer-lopez-iggy-azalea/ | | |
| **BONUS:** https://music.yahoo.com/blogs/music-news/miley-cyrus-reveals-twerk-replacing-dance-down-under-164547793.html | | |

**Brief Analysis:** Hip Hop and the black American women within it have long been criticized for their bodies and how they do not easily fulfill existing Western standards of beauty.[8] Yet, fast-forwarding several years, it appears non-black women are glamorized when they approach black beauty standards and profit from it. Lip injections anyone?

**Bonus Analysis:** This article actually ascribes cultural ownership to Miley Cyrus — as if she really woke up one day last week and created a new dance that she "revealed." She merely imitated what others have done and is better positioned within the mainstream to leverage credit for it.

| APPROPRIATION Example #2 | | |
|---|---|---|
| **Agents** | **Artifact** | **Approach** |
| Daniel Radcliffe & Jimmy Fallon | Element of Emcee | National pop culture stage on "Late Night with Jimmy Fallon" television show |
| **LINK:** https://www.youtube.com/watch?v=aKdV5FvXLuI | | |
| **BONUS LINK:** https://www.youtube.com/watch?v=ivUu5hyocO4 | | |

**Brief Analysis:** "Harry Potter" star Radcliffe received much attention for his cover or rendition of Blackalicious' "Alphabet Aerobics" (profiled in Chapter 5, "Demonstration") as the links above will show. But what you will not find is the emcee from Blackalicious (recall his name?) himself receiving national television exposure performing his craft. In other words, not only until such craft is mediated through white male fame does the intellectual feat now become interesting. This makes Radcliffe "look cool" and shows that he has "range" outside of Quidditch matches.

| APPROPRIATION Example #3 | | |
|---|---|---|
| **Agent** | **Artifact** | **Approach** |
| Lifetime TV channel | Blacks without dark skin | National cable television show, "Alliyah: The Princess of R&B" |
| **LINK:** http://www.theroot.com/blogs/the_grapevine/2014/08/dear_lifetime_how_does_one_cast_a_light_skinned_skinny_missy_elliott_timbaland.html?wpisrc=obinsite | | |

**Brief Analysis:** Complaints swirled around Lifetime's casting decisions, namely, to have skinny, fair-skinned actors take the roles of Missy Elliot and Timbaland just to be more appealing to a majority white audience.

| APPROPRIATION Example #4 | | |
|---|---|---|
| **Agent** | **Artifact** | **Approach** |
| Katy Perry | Black hairstyle (cornrows) | National distributed music video, "This Is How We Do" |
| **LINK:** https://www.youtube.com/watch?v=7RMQksXpQSk | | |
| **BONUS:** https://www.youtube.com/watch?v=O1KJRRSB_XA | | |
| **DOUBLE BONUS:** https://www.youtube.com/watch?v=E0CazRHB0so#t=124 | | |

**Brief Analysis:** Katy Perry apparently is an "equal opportunist" and dressed up as a Japanese Geisha during the 2013 American Music Awards to the tune of some controversy. Whatever feedback Ms. Perry received was not a full deterrent as she subsequently donned cornrows and is depicted eating watermelon in the video "This Is How We Do." The cornrows hairstyle is created by and used primarily by members of the black community or anyone else able to use it based upon hair texture. But perhaps, Ms. Perry felt it was "no big deal."

**Bonus Analysis:** Amandla Stenberg (likely best known as the character Rue in the first "Hunger Games" movie — why just the first movie? — uh, we digress) posted a short, sub-five minute video on YouTube entitled "Don't Cash Crop on My Cornrows." Out of the mouth of babes...

**Double Bonus Analysis:** British songstress Lily Allen came under fire for "ironic racism" displayed through her "Hard Out Here" video released in 2013. Allen claims she was satirizing the larger idea of female objectification, but as it turns out, she was the only female fully dressed on screen and had an overwhelming majority of scantily-clad black bodies twerking their gluteal muscles (in slow motion) to make her point.

One must watch the video to independently investigate the truth for themselves, but in so doing, do consider whether Allen ironically re-created and re-presented the very imagery that perhaps she was attempting to critique. Read further to see Allen's reasons for not appearing in less clothing alongside the dancers — a pre-meditated decision that was contemplated beforehand — and whether that adequately explains the decision to use the (Rap Music culture's) twerking aesthetic of black female bodies as the gratuitous, shorthand examples of societal and systematic decay.

## APPROPRIATION Example #5

| Agent | Artifact | Approach |
|-------|----------|----------|
| Taylor Swift | Blackness | National distributed music video, "Shake it Off" |
| **LINK:** https://www.youtube.com/watch?v=nfWlot6h_JM | | |
| **BONUS:** http://www.cnn.com/2015/01/29/living/feat-taylor-swift-trademarks/index.html | | |

**Brief Analysis:** Ms. Swift appears to adopt a similar strategy as Ms. Allen, only she appears to be infiinitely more successful at it. With over 1.2 billion views on YouTube, Ms. Swift immediately at the 0:18 mark inserts herself within "Rap Music Culture" aesthetics. She can only go so far as to change her dress and poses, but she employed others to display the other aspects of the culture through dance and oversized boom boxes.

At the 2:09 mark, Ms. Swift too, cannot resist the allure of the twerking resplendent gluteal muscles of the black female body as she crawls underneath in awe and admiration, carefully, as her neck is laden with several gold chains.

**Bonus Analysis.** Swift also wishes not to let others capitalize off Hip Hop culture and leave her behind (no pun intended), so she has acted to trademark the phrase: "this sick beat" so that the common people who invented it and used it for free can now pay her to use it again in the near future. "Sick" in this instance is slang for "cool." How sick is that?

## APPROPRIATION Example #6

| Agent | Artifact | Approach |
|-------|----------|----------|
| Iggy Azalea | Blackness | National distributed music album |
| **LINK:** http://www.theroot.com/articles/culture/2014/06/whites_in_hip_hop_why_music_by_iggy_azalea_and_others_is_so_popular_and.2.html | | |

**Brief Analysis:** Australian-born performer Iggy Azalea took the mainstream by storm and flew up the charts, but not without a bit of turbulence. Members from within the Hip Hop community, notably Azaleia Banks and Q-Tip of A Tribe Called Quest, publicly criticized Ms. Azalea for appropriation.[9] Interestingly enough, Iggy's response did not respond to the critique, but instead criticized Ms. Banks' character. Her founding producer, rapper T.I. initially defended her, raising questions over the sincerity of his defense since it may be pure business savvy to defend the person with whom you are making hundreds of thousands of dollars. T.I. since publicly backed down from that supportive position, citing concerns with Azalea's real affection for Hip Hop.[10] Speaking of real, Azalea has since admitted that her appearance was partly manufactured with respect to breast augmentation and nose reduction surgery although she insists her derrier is authentic.[11] Apart and aside from her appearance, many within the Hip Hop community have raised questions concerning the authenticity of Azalea's style. Azalea is fully accepted as a marketable pop culture commodity within the mainstream, and is cloaked and clad with her officially black paramour in NBA player Nick Young (aka Swaggy P) and former mentor, rapper T.I., who helped put her on the map. This might be fine for the industry of Rap Music. But this has nothing to do with the heritage of Hip Hop.

## APPROPRIATION Example #7

| Agent | Artifact | Approach |
|---|---|---|
| Rap Battle | Hip Hop culture, generally | Humorous "rap battle" between Disney characters Snow White and Princess Elsa ("Frozen") |
| **LINK:** https://www.youtube.com/watch?v=gcrQvoCzs80 ||| 

**Brief Analysis:** As the subject of numerous vines, videos, jokes, memes, etc., the public definitely maintains a fascination with Hip Hop. Some "rap battles" posted online are quite clever[12] and quite popular. But still, similar to the Radcliffe/Blackalicious analysis, we must interrogate why the original black and brown versions are not as popular as the white reimaginings of what Hip Hop culture should look like. For this example, note how this video, despite lacking A-list, household name talent, still is able to muster an eye-popping **78 MILLION VIEWS**. In contrast to the glamorized white female "princess" model, would a rap battle between two black "icons" (e.g., Rosa Parks vs Harriet Tubman???) be as popular?

## APPROPRIATION Example #8

| Agent | Artifact | Approach |
|---|---|---|
| Katie Couric | Black Dancing | Nationally syndicated news reel |
| **LINK:** https://www.youtube.com/watch?v=8kt1VpVt228; http://news.yahoo.com/video/lil-buck-teaches-katie-couric-153625282.html |||

**Brief Analysis:** Here, appropriation is taking place, but in a more subtle way. The benefit is to Couric's professional career and personal reputation. By attempting to engage in such (Hip Hop) dance moves that are normally "foreign" to her, she hopefully gains new audiences. The focus of the feature is Couric, her reactions and feelings about the dance move. Reporting on white-dominated "square dancing" may not be considered as exciting a topic for national reporting for Couric's team — perhaps it is the contrast of genders, cultures and race that keep the viewer's interest in the minds of the producers.

## APPROPRIATION Example #9

| Agent | Artifact | Approach |
|-------|----------|----------|
| Seattle Symphony | Hip Hop culture, generally | Official performance in concert with Sir Mix-a-Lot of arguably his most famous hit, "Baby Got Back" |
| **LINK:** http://www.nytimes.com/2014/06/11/arts/music/debating-the-seattle-orchestras-foray-with-sir-mix-a-lot.html?_r=0; https://www.youtube.com/watch?v=w59e20ijOpE | | |
| **BONUS LINK:** http://news.yahoo.com/blogs/trending-now/family-turns--baby-got-back--into-back-to-school-anthem-194845952.html | | |

**Brief Analysis:** A simple Google search will reveal the pearl-clutching and hand-wringing that accompanied the release of Sir Mix-A-Lot's track, "Baby Got Back." The video was not only risqué (in the pre-twerking era), but it was also emblematic of the unchecked black licentiousness that would corrupt "our" future generations. Years later, after being fully appropriated, mostly only whites play the song at professional sporting events and weddings, etc. (see the Bonus Link for just one of many examples, two decades after the fact). The Seattle Symphony's "rendition" of this iconic song is no different.

## APPROPRIATION Example #10

| Agent | Artifact | Approach |
|-------|----------|----------|
| Hoodie Allen | Hip Hop, specifically | Nationally released album |
| **LINK:** http://www.hoodieallen.com/music/ | | |

**Brief Analysis:** No further comment.

# BEFORE YOU BOUNCE

- **FEATURES:** whites within mainstream channels have a solid and consistent history of first marginalizing and ostracizing blacks, then when blacks do something to compensate for the pain and create their own expression, whites then cautiously observe and criticize initially, only to grow fanatic and appropriate it for themselves later. Then the final stage is when mainstream participants utilize resources to study "it," reproduce "it" themselves and then sell it back to the people they appropriated "it" from with whites now at the center. The previous chapter pages contain but a few examples.

- **KNOW:** the three parts required for Appropriation

- Examples are endless, but if you wish to check out a "breakdancing conversation" between Late Night host Jimmy Fallon and A-list Hollywood actor Brad Pitt, here goes: http://m.youtube.com/watch?v=wBij_rEXdCk

- The comedy troupe of the nationally televised "Saturday Night Live" recognized and burlesqued this Appropriation concept by producing a skit that purported to be "an authentic biography" of "The Jay Z Story"...starring white Irish actor, Mike O'Brien: http://www.youtube.com/watch?v=lzg9Iu0uEeg&sns=em

# 10

# SUMMATION

# TIME TO FLIP THE SCRIPT

Just like a turntable revolving on a set, we now conclude by returning full circle to one of our key beginning points — namely that Hip Hop **"started out with a broad palette of themes but has increasingly evolved into a medium for worshipping misogyny, materialism and murder."**[1] Let us consider each of the frequently asserted knocks (or criticisms) expressed in mainstream culture against Hip Hop:

| 3 F.A.K.E. M.C.s vs. Hip Hop | | |
|---|---|---|
| Misogyny | Materialism | Mayhem |

## Misogyny/Sex

What exactly are we criticizing here? If it is the objectification of women, then let's get started! For all we have to do is start campaiging against our primetime television and at our local movie theater and supermarket check out counters and grow from there. Projection may be at play here. From "Big Bang Theory" to "Desperate Housewives," there is hardly a single primetime show that **DOES NOT** invoke or involve sex or sexual themes. And so it follows, that there is many a Rap Music video that invokes or involves sex or sexual themes. But notice, we said Rap Music.

While our Hip Hop umbrellas largely shield us from those who wax philosphically about "making it rain," or throwing so much money in the air at the half naked women on the stripper poles that it appears that it is "raining" money, we must point out one inconsistency. Mainstream critics condemn the black and brown male who frequents and patronizes the misogynistic strip club, but not the white man who built and owns and operates it.

Poor black and brown people did not pass legislation allowing for the minutiae of "sitting, no touching" in strip clubs. Poor black and brown people did not make prostitution legal (Nevada). Poor black and brown people do not control or own most of the billion dollar pornography industry. Nor do poor black and brown people own most our nation's "breasturants."[2] Poor black and brown people do not own most of the strip clubs (of which there are plenty) in our nation. Strip clubs exist because this is how a significant portion of white males "conduct business" by virtue of "entertaining."[3]

Yet, the minute that poor black and brown people hint that they too, wish to approach this line as part of a fantasy — whether misguided or not — to extract pleasure out of an otherwise miserable existence, then they are to be demonized? Or, more succinctly stated, when poor black and browns attempt to stylize themselves in a sexually liberated manner, are we upset because in some abstract sense they dare to be "white"? If not, and if **WE** truly wish to clean up our act for the children's sake,[4] then let's be consistent and clean up misogyny in all of its pervasive forms and not just target Hip Hop (of which Rap Music is largely culpable). What follows are just a couple **RISQUÉ EXAMPLES** found within other sectors of mainstream society in the form of print advertisement, television commercial and hit song:

| JUST A COUPLE RISQUÉ EXAMPLES | |
|---|---|
| **LINK:** http://finance.yahoo.com/news/american-apparels-provocative-back-school-172412765.html | **ANALYSIS:** While showcased primarily in its overseas United Kingdom campaign, Los Angeles based clothier, *American Apparel*, landed in a bit of hot water for its "provocative" ads showcasing "back to school" skirts targeted towards teenagers by faceless models bent over with their backs to the camera thereby exposing their colorfully patterned undergarments. Some families might object to their daughters skirting conventional norms of attire that promote more modesty over the sharing of additional information underneath their teenage skirts. |

## JUST A COUPLE RISQUÉ EXAMPLES

| | |
|---|---|
| **LINK:** https://www.youtube.com/watch?v=WlUvQkW4B1k | **ANALYSIS:** This *Carl's Jr.* hamburger ad first ran during Super Bowl XLIX in 2015. Plenty of eyes saw it seeing how the Super Bowl is the most heavily watched show in all of America.[5] Here, Charlotte McKinney is the subject of male gaze and is intimated to be intimately naked, or "au naturel" (the name of the burger advertised) as she walks the street. In ironic contrast where the exposure of Janet Jackson's dark nipple caused a national affront,[6] the producers of this ad cleverly showed the maximum amount of McKinney's white breasts to get their point accross. Some families might object to the messaging that women are to be oogled at as a piece of juicy meat as an object of sexual desire (especially if buxom and blonde) by other males while selling juicy meat (au naturel, that is). |
| **LINK:** https://www.youtube.com/watch?v=KlyXNRrsk4A | **ANALYSIS:** In what can be characterized as a "fun" song & video "Last Friday Night (T.G.I.F.)," pop star and teen queen Katy Perry does include in the chorus (@ 3:00 mark) the following lyrics: "We went streaking in the park, skinny dipping in the dark, then we had a ménage à trois, last Friday night." Not to sound prude, but some families might object to their teenagers facilitating ménage à trois, or sexual intercourse between three people. "Innocent" middle & high schoolers do constitute a significant portion of her fan base as "Last Friday Night" comes from the 2010 album entitled "Teenage Dream." No "Parental Advisory" label applied to the album. |

We cannot "pick and choose," what represents misogyny in our society for our inconsistency will open us up to claims of bias. In the foregoing examples, risky (or risqué) sexual themes are ever-present, but are simply stylized in a manner that the mainstream public (translation: white majority) deems acceptable. Are aspects of Hip Hop misogynistic? Absolutely! But as a dependent subculture within Mother America, we must consider the source; Hip Hop did not invent misogyny, nor should it be the sole scapegoat for it.

## Materialism/Money

What exactly are we criticizing here? Why are we so quick to judge and criticize the glamorization of capital acquisition within a capitalistic society? Recall, we said Hip Hop does not come straight from the beaches of Malibu. Hence, we cannot overlook that the overwhelming majority of those who create, practice and live Hip Hop are largely lacking or without — or at least, started off that way. If James Baldwin is correct in asserting that one is "born, then suffers, then dies,"[7] then what is the expected reaction of one who faced obstacles all their life and managed to achieve (not modest, but outstanding) financial success? Happiness perhaps?

Let us consider the major lottery winner who fails to smile — why would they not? Celebrating is rational. Moreover, significant capital symbolizes acceptance, place and **VALUE** in society — for clearly the person is doing something right with their life in order to be financially prosperous — or appear that way, if only for the video.

Do the poor criticize Hip Hop? Or is Hip Hop criticized by those who can afford to do so? Very rarely do we scrutinize the daily decisions of the rich — $1,200 trashcans notwithstanding.[8] But yet, on this stage, we critique those wanting to leap frog from underclass to upper class status without paying homage to middle class mores in between. Yet, we celebrate the rich constantly — whether it be through television shows like "MTV Cribs" or Red Carpet profiles during the Academy Awards[9] — just not when it features black and brown faces within the field of Hip Hop. The young men flashing their little jewelry, clothes and cars — **THEY** are the misguided lot who overesteem material possessions and run the risk of corrupting others with their shallow ethos. **FIDDLESTICKS & POPPYCOCK!**[10] We must be mindful when criticizing the consumers and not the producers.

## Mayhem/Power

What exactly are we criticizing here? This last piece is a bit more difficult, for very few of us can sensibly justify violence towards another. So we will not attempt to do so here. In the name of consistency, respect for fellow persons is a universal standard we urge us all to maintain. We earlier defined Mayhem as including, but not limited to: violence (including murder), anti-authority, rejection of middle class mores and glamorization of drug use. Of the three prongs of the American Dream Triple Team, this third prong is arguably the most solid in contrast to the more hypocritical stances taken against the other two. Real talk, as they say.

Our offering is this: as Hip Hop is a dependent subculture of larger American culture, the genre at the very least cannot be criticized for creating **MORE** mayhem than what already exists.[8] Hip Hop can be criticized for glorifying violence just like Hollywood can, to the extent that our society feels violence is not necessary (or entertaining) in all instances to help us navigate our daily affairs. The only salvo offered here will be the reminder that many members of the Hip Hop community have been victimized by violence — from outside their community. Whether directly, from what they perceive to be inconsistent policing tactics (i.e., anti-authority) or indirectly from national news coverage about a person with whom they identify (think: Sandra Bland), processing these different forms of violence requires a constructive outlet to maintain sanity. While some undoubtedly approach and cross "the line," many utilize their "poetic license" with Demonstrations to signify as Dr. Henry Louis Gates would remind us, or metaphorically express what they cannot or should not express in literal terms when not rapping on the record. This salvo does not excuse nor exonerate, but merely explicates many Hip Hop practitioners' frequently frustrated quest for power.

# ESCAPEGOAT

Notice how the American Dream Triple Team "just happens" to align with the three frequently asserted knocks (or criticisms) expressed in mainstream culture against Hip Hop. Such an alignment raises the question of what exactly are we criticizing here? Hip Hop unto itself? Or the ills of a larger American society as projected on to and manifested through Hip Hop?

| American Dream Triple Team | | |
|---|---|---|
| Sex | Money | Power |
| 3 F.A.K.E. M.C.s | | |
| Misogyny | Materialism | Mayhem |

In effect, in publicly casting aspersions upon Hip Hop as being Misogynist, Materialistic and full of Mayhem, what is being said is that Hip Hop is of no redeeming, long-standing value in society.[11] We patently reject the premise of this anti-intellectualist stance for we simply know better.[12]

Hip Hop is portrayed in a negative light because it is an easy target to scapegoat. Is all of Hip Hop perfect? No. Does it embody themes of misogyny and materialism and violence or mayhem? Absolutely. But, as a subculture responding to dominant culture, it is often easy to overlook that American culture and Hollywood embody these themes all the more so. Misogyny existed before Hip Hop did. Hollywood objectifies women **EVERY NIGHT** on our TV screens, but yet, Hip Hop videos conveniently become the scourge of our society. As a relatively independent, nonwhite dominated outlet outside of mainstream media, Hip Hop is subject to more intense scrutiny and criticism due to Hip Hop's ability to dispassionately critique aspects of American culture that are inconsistent, especially when it comes to issues of social justice. But rather than exert and invest the necessary effort to be more consistent in society as a whole on matters of Misogyny, Materialism and Mayhem, the easier route is to blame Hip Hop as the singular source rather than understand Hip Hop as another resource with which to understand our society.[13]

# PEACE & RESPECT

If anything, after considering "the elements" and HipHopetypes together, closer analysis reveals an extremely complex, substantively rich and stimulating dynamic that challenges both practioners and patrons alike to continue to struggle for humanity. The struggle for humanity in America for nonwhite persons is made more complicated by the overarching presence of the Unholy Trinity and its stubbornly persistent themes of Romantic Racialism, Femininity and Negrophobia. The influential "rags to riches" Horatio Alger myth adds another layer of pressure as individuals strive to succeed in society — with success often defined as material acquisitions or lifestyle accommodations that come in at exorbitantly high prices.

Hip Hop, when properly understood and applied, is an antidote to the destructive forces of the Unholy Trinity that work systematically and institutionally to isolate individuals and suppress their creativity. The six consistent HipHopetypes provide a common foundation by which people can come together as a community and build through the constant channeling of creative energies for a common good. Misdirected Rap Artists identify with questionable mainstream values in the same way hostages sometimes identify with their captors.[14] Yet, Hip Hop is the continued creative collaboration for humanity or rather, the quest for peace and respect with peace and respect.

It has been said earlier that Hip Hop created a multi-verse (get it?) as opposed to a universe. Within this realm, one may enjoy and patronize Rap Music. This is all well and good. This manuscript was not composed to oppose all things Rap Music. But just be clear not to confuse Rap Music with Hip Hop. While an open ended question for reflection, we nonetheless provide a simple, one-part test:

| Simple, 1-Part Hip Hop vs. Rap Music Test |
|---|
| How OFTEN and how OBVIOUS is reverence & reference made to The Elements and HipHopetypes? |

Quite simply, if the track is devoid of that which constitutes Hip Hop, then the track shall be called by some other name. Careful study reveals that as an antidote to the Unholy Trinity, Hip Hop prompts the practioner and patron alike to consider larger questions of significant philosophical meaning:

| Hiphopetype | Epistemological Question at Issue |
|---|---|
| Rejection | Who refuses my existence? |
| Prescription | What to do? |
| Aspiration | When in the future will it happen? |
| Description | Where are matters currently? |
| Demonstration | What do I do to exist/persist? |
| Recognition | How did we come to be? |

These epistemological issues cannot be taken lightly. This is the mistake of mainstream media critics that sloppily advance only superficial critiques and fail to penetrate the literal meaning for larger meaning. While Rap Music is very much commercialized and commodified, Hip Hop was not born that way. Hip Hop was created as a means of survival. If man's inhumanity to man precipitated conditions whereby many were marginalized and oppressed — for no logical reason other than race — then Hip Hop as an antidote represents man's humanity to man as a condition for freedom.

# HEROIC EFFORT

The HipHopetypes, when taken together, metaphorically represent the soul of the collective Hip Hop community following the "Hero Journey" monomyth with Rejection starting the quest for humanity.[15]

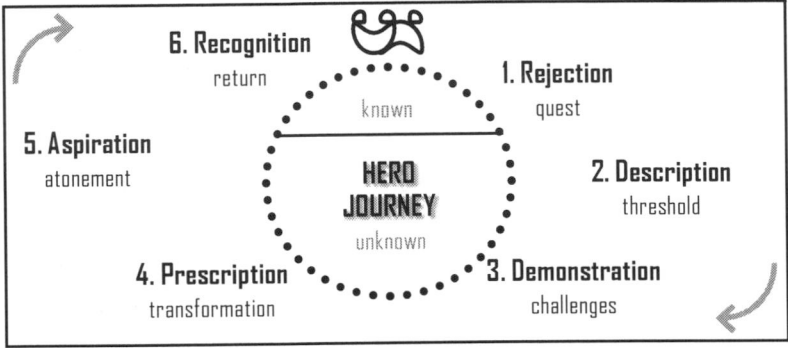

In essence, Hip Hop (or **HIPHOPOLOGY**) works collectively to generate the positive powers of **FAITH** and **FACILITATION** (as evidence of creativity) to combat the polarizing powers of **FEAR** and **FASCINATION**.

| Rejection | Description | Demonstration | Prescription | Aspiration | Recognition |
|---|---|---|---|---|---|
| HipHopetypes Corresponding with Honored Hip Hop Elements | | | | | |
| MC | DJ | Graffiti | Knowledge of Self | B-boy/girl | ALL |
| Unholy Trinity Antidote to the Corresponding Anti-Creative Forces | | | | | |
| FEAR | | | FASCINATION | | |
| exclusion | delusion | marginalization | indecision | desolation | invalidation |
| HipHopetypes' Ethos as Evidence of Creative GENIUS | | | | | |
| FAITH | | | FACILITATION | | |
| inclusion | clarity | empowerment | wisdom | optimism | dignity & respect |

Given the difficulty present in achieving the American Dream as a privileged white individual, let alone as a marginalized nonwhite individual, Hip Hop has put forth a heroic effort thus far indeed.

# AND IT SOUNDS SO NICE...

In conclusion, what do we make of this force entitled Hip Hop? When making the assertion that "Hip Hop is **GENIUS**," we seek not to be redundant, but merely reassuring in repeating a refrain issued earlier — think of it as a chorus or hook that appears more than once within a track! Quite simply, our operating definition of **GENIUS** is "the ability to generate and create that which is particularly intelligent, insightful or inspirational." The locus of our working definition is rooted in the ability to channel creative forces for a greater purpose. After all, destructive forces are ever present. For instance, our bodies specifically fight decay on a daily basis. Thus, we view creation as the opposite of destruction and the **GENIUS** within us all represents the innate ability to fight for that which is best in life.

To confuse commercial Rap Music made by a few artists with how Hip-Hop is actually lived by millions is to miss the power that Hip-Hop produces.[16] Such a conflation suggests that when such musical vibrations are not as politically potent or intellectually substantive, they become more acceptable within the mainstream as Rap Music. It bears repeating, that as a quasi-independent source of income outside of the mainstream, Hip Hop itself represents independence.

Above all, one should "know their audience" as the main criticisms of Hip Hop come from sources outside the culture. Yet, Hip Hop has taken on an incredible journey; that which started off counter-culture now **IS** mainstream culture. Hip Hop tracks spin on turntables like the Earth does on its axis, literally looping in sounds and themes, recycling style and ideas while reinventing itself (fresh!). What started as "two turntables and a mic" by silenced people in forgotten ghettoes has the whole world listening and remembering.

And that my friends, is **GENIUS**...

# A
PPENDIX

# NOTATION

MLA Style

## Chapter Zero References, pp. 2-8

**1.** See generally: a) Chang, Jeff. Can't Stop Won't Stop: A History of the Hip Hop Generation. New York: Picador, 2005; b) Dyson, Michael. Know What I Mean?: Reflections on Hip-Hop. New York: Basic Civitas, 2010; c) Kitwana, Bakari. The Hip-Hop Generation: Young Blacks and the Crisis in African-American Culture. New York: Basic Civitas, 2003.

**2.** "Of all the music styles to emerge in the last 50 years, none took the world by storm quite like hip-hop, said researchers Wednesday who tracked pop's evolution with cold, hard stats." "Mathematics Tracks the Hip Hop 'Revolution.'" *The Tico Times*. The Tico Times, 6 May 2015. Web. 12 December 2015. <http://www.ticotimes.net/2015/05/06/mathematics-tracks-the-hip-hop-revolution>.

**3.** Reference to controversial statement and title of 2006 album, "Hip Hop Is Dead" by Nas.

**4.** Hip Hop is and has been a billion dollar industry. Note the date of this citation. Watson, Julie. "Rapper's Delight: A Billion Dollar Industry." *Forbes*. Forbes, 18 February 2004. Web. 12 December 2015. < http://www.forbes.com/2004/02/18/cx_jw_0218hiphop.html>.

**5.** Katz, Gregory. "Rap's Impact Outweighs Influence of The Beatles, Says Scientific Study." *Billboard*. Yahoo! Music, 6 May, 2015. 12 December 2015. <https://www.yahoo.com/music/raps-impact-outweighs-influence-of-the-beatles-118315147221.html>.

**6.** Two turn tables and a mic(rophone) are symbolic of the essential, most basic equipment any practioner of Hip Hop would require to rock a set. Of course, electricity is not required in order for the forces of Hip Hop to be properly channeled, but is very useful when seeking to be amplified. Within Hip Hop circles, this familiar phrasing was famously commemorated by Buckshot Shorty in 1999 with a song so entitled. After repeating "two turntables on the mic," Buckshot reminded us: "One phat emcee on the set!"

**7.** Reference to 1990 song "The Mission" by Flatbush's own Special Ed.

## Chapter 1 References, pp. 10-20

**1.** "Rap and hip-hop music have roots in the griot tradition." Turck, Mary C. Freedom Song: Young Voices and the Struggle for Civil Rights. Chicago: Chicago Review Press, 2008, p. 23.

**2.** Manifest Destiny is defined as "the right of America to 'conquer, colonize, and Christianize' the continent of North America." Buck, Christopher. Religious Myths and Visions of America: How Minority Faiths Redefined America's World Role. Westport, CT: Praeger Publishers, 2009, p. 8.

**3.** See generally, Ignatiev, Noel. How the Irish Became White. New York: Routledge, 2009.

**4.** "Another force involved in creating and maintaining ethnicity is the degree of identifiability of members of a subpopulation. To be targets of discrimination, members of a subpopulation need to be visible and readily identified. And so, the more distinctive members of a subpopulation are, the more likely they are to become targets of discrimination." Aguirre, Jr., Adalberto and Johnathan H. Turner. American Ethnicity: The Dynamics and Consequences of Discrimination. New York: McGraw-Hill, 2011, p. 44.

**5.** The term "and women" is largely a euphemism for "white women." See generally, Sana Loue, Martha Sajatovic, eds. Encyclopedia of Women's Health. New York: Kluwer Academic/Plenum Publishers, 2004, p. 264: "To speak of feminism in the context of a set of overarching ideals that define a unified movement is a misrepresentation.... Radical feminism and its numerous branches primarily represent a movement focused on issues defined by white women, rendering women of color invisible." Thus, while historically suppressed and subjugated relative to white men, white women nonetheless enjoy a privileged position in relation to virtually all other racial/gender demographics by virtue of their special "in-house" relationship with white men as the mothers, daughters, wives, etc. of white men. Thus, while we may not think of it this way, white women are frequently the direct beneficiaries and targets of white male prowess and consequently are uniquely positioned to leverage their privileged status for equality with other white men.

In contrast to white men's occasional acquiesence to white female sexuality, white men have historically demonstrated an extreme reluctance to be beholden to or subordinate to black male masculinity. If anything, white males have demonstrated a desire to mute black male sexuality and power in the presence of white males. When white males make an exception to their masculinity being usurped, this is typically when they allow themselves self-deprecation in the presence of (usually, more attractive) white women.

Again, we must be careful, for the common phrasing "blacks and women" virtually silences the presence of black women who suffer from ironic invisibility based upon their intersectionality of both black race and female gender identities. While we have other business to attend, it is imperative to recognize that "women" is not an inclusive term and actually becomes a coded euphemism for "white women," for that is who practically has such access to the existing white-dominated power structure in America and who the male-dominated power structure has a vested interest in placating. White men in power, even if only acting out of their own self interest, realize that it is not feasibly sustainable for them to be dominant and exclusive in all professional affairs, when white women are included within their personal affairs in so many ways. The question then becomes what incentive exists for white males in power to make such accommodations for those outside of their inner circle — especially among race and gender lines. Good luck to black and brown males.

**6.** See Chapter 10, "Left Behind." Longworth, Richard C. Caught in the Middle: America's Heartland in the Age of Globalism. New York: Bloomsbury, 2008.

**7.** Silverblatt, Art. Jane Ferry, Barbara Finan. Approaches to Media Literacy: A Handbook. New York: Routledge, 2009, p.205.

**8**. Bialik, Carl. "Is the Conventional Wisdom Correct in Measuring Hip Hop Audience?" Wall Street Journal Online. *Wall Street Journal*, 5 May, 2005. Web. 12 December, 2015. < http://www.wsj.com/articles/SB111521814339424546>.

**9**. Landrum, Jr., Jonathan. "Lamar Says Swift's Remarks Help Himself, Hip-Hop." Associated Press. *Yahoo! Music*. 14 September, 2014. Web. 12 December, 2015 < https://www.yahoo.com/music/s/lamar-says-swifts-remarks-help-himself-hip-hop-062303659.html?nf=1>.

**10**. "Historians have long been aware that many southerners proclaimed slavery a necessary evil before the 1820s." Tallant, Harold D. Evil Necessity: Slavery and Political Culture in Antebellum Kentucky. Lexington: University Press of Kentucky, 2003, p.4.

**11**. Mink, Gwendolyn; Alice O'Connor. Poverty in the United States: An Encyclopedia of History, Politics, and Policy, Volume 1. Santa Barbara, CA: ABC-CLIO, Inc., 2004.

**12**. In Thomas Jefferson's "original rough draught" of the Declaration of Independence, he analogizes the relationship between Britain and its taxation policies of the American colonies as akin to slavery. "Declaring Independence: Drafting the Documents." *Library of Congress*. Web. 12 December 2015. < https://www.loc.gov/exhibits/declara/ruffdrft.html>. This passage was later replaced with a more ambiguous passage about the-then King George's attempt to incite "domestic insurrections among us," primarily through unfair taxation policies.

**13**. See Chapter Four, "Uncle Tom and the Anglo-Saxons: Romantic Racialism in the North." Fredrickson, George. The Black Image in the White Mind: The Debate on Afro-American Character and Destiny, 1817-1914. New York: Harper & Row, 1971.

**14**. Id., p. 114.

**15**. Id., Chapter Nine, "Negro as Beast: Southern Negrophobia at the Turn of the Century."

**16**. "Lynching in America: Confronting the Legacy of Racial Terror," Equal Justice Initiative. *Equal Justice Initiative*, 2015. Web. 12 December, 2015. < http://www.eji.org/files/EJI%20Lynching%20in%20America%20SUMMARY.pdf>.

Also, see by Cynthia Skove Nevels, Lynching to Belong: Claiming Whiteness through Racial Violence. Centennial Series of the Association of Former Students, Texas A&M University, 2007. With case studies of lynchings fueled by early Irish and Italian immigrants, the premise offered is that the more racist outside immigration groups were, the more they proved their "Americanness" for mainstream inclusion.

**17**. Bykofsky, Melissa. "What's Happening in Your Brain and Body as You Listen to Music. Yahoo! Health. *Yahoo!*, 3 November, 2015. Web. 12 December 2015 <https://www.yahoo.com/health/what-s-happening-in-your-1291460065820726.html>.

**18**. "When you exercise, your muscles use more energy. Your heart must beat faster to supply them with the oxygen they need to produce that energy." Ergo, when one's heart beats faster, they have more energy, and with more energy, one has more capacity to move "faster" as opposed to if the individual's body was at rest. Miller, Joe. "Why Does Exercise Make Your Heart Rate Go Up?" Demand Media. *AZ Central*, n.d. Web. 12 December, 2015. < http://healthyliving.azcentral.com/exercise-make-heart-rate-up-7931.html>.

**19.** "Another notable characteristic of our bodies is that it is not only the ear that reacts to sound: in proximity to a loudspeaker or a subwoofer, which sends low notes at a high volume, our intestines vibrate." Volk, Carol. Extremely Loud: Sound as a Weapon. New York: The New Press, 2013, Chapter 1.

**20.** A well known phrase in the Declaration of Independence that was misspelled and served as the title of a famous "rags to riches" story of Michael Gardner, as personified by Will Smith in the movie so entitled as "Pursuit of Happyness."

**21.** Sadler, Roger L. Electronic Media Law. Thousand Oaks, CA: Sage Publications, Inc., 2005, p. 286.

**22.** Blanchard, Margaret A. Revolutionary Sparks: Freedom of Expression in Modern America. New York: Oxford University Press, 1992, p. 474.

**23.** Staples, Brent. "How Hip-Hop Music Lost Its Way and Betrayed Its Fans." The Opinion Pages. *The New York Times.* 12 May, 2005. Web. 12 December 2015. < http://www.nytimes.com/2005/05/12/opinion/how-hiphop-music-lost-its-way-and-betrayed-its-fans.html?_r=0>.

## Chapter 2 References, pp. 22-32

**1.** Mitchell, Tony. Global Noise: Rap and Hip Hop Outside the USA. Middletown, CT: Wesleyan University Press, 2001.

**2.** Watson, Julie. "Rapper's Delight: A Billion Dollar Industry."

**3.** Peterson, James Braxton. "Rewriting the Remix: College Composition and the Educational Elements of Hip Hop" in Schooling Hip-Hop: Expanding Hip-Hop Based Education Across the Curriculum. New York: Teachers College Press, 2013, p. 47-48.

**4.** "What Is the Zulu Nation???????" *Universal Zulu Nation.* n.d. Web. 12 December, 2015. < http://www.zulunation.com/about-zulunation/.

**5.** Schloss, Joseph G. Making Beats: The Art of Sample-Based Hip-Hop. Middletown, CT: Wesleyan University Press, 2004.

**6.** Visit "The Notorious IBE" or International Breakdance Event website to gain a feel for what's out there: http://www.thenotoriousibe.com/.

**7.** Lovata, Troy R. and Elizabeth Olton, eds. Understanding Graffiti: Multidisciplinary Studies from the Prehistory to the Present. Walnut Creek, CA: Left Coast Press, Inc., 2015.

**8.** Id.

**9.** Olsen, Brad. Modern Esoteric: Beyond Our Senses. San Francisco, CA: CCC Publishing, 2014.

## Chapter 3 References, pp. 34-44

1. "The nature of human life is that people tend to live and associate in groups." Milligan, Ian and Irene Stevens. Residential Child Care: Collaborative Practice. Thousand Oaks, CA: SAGE Publications, Inc., 2006, p. 64.

2. "Representatives and direct Taxes shall be apportioned among the several States which may be included within this Union, according to their respective Numbers, which shall be determined by adding to the whole Number of free Persons, including those bound to Service for a Term of Years, and excluding Indians not taxed, three fifths of all other Persons." United States Constitution. Art. I, Sec. 2, Cl. 3.

3. "The one-drop rule was crucial to maintaining Jim Crow segregation" where the most minimal of linkages to African or black lineage would determine their life chances and extent of protection from strictly observed segregationist laws "reinforced by extralegal threats and terrorism" for "alleged violations of the master-servant ettiquete — for 'getting out of their place.'" F. James Davis, "Black Identity in the United States" in Multiculturalism in the United States: Current Issues, Contemporary Voices, Peter Kivisto and Georganne Rundblad, eds. Thousand Oaks, CA: Pine Forge Press, 2000, pp. 102-103.

4. Economically restrictive laws designed to advantage white labor in the "free market economy" were numerous in the periods during and immediately following the formal end to the Era of Enslavement. Examples include the 1833 Kentucky Licensing Prohibition which forbade free persons of color from obtaining business licenses and the 1845 Georgia Contracting Law which prohibited contracts with black mechanics. See Appendix of Claud Anderson, Black Labor, White Wealth: The Search for Power and Economic Justice. Bethesda, MD: PowerNomics Corporation of America, 1994.

5. The University of Chicago conducted a study entitled "Are Emily and Brendan More Employable than Lakisha and Jamal?" with the finding that white-sounding names are 50% more likely to get called back for an initial interview than identical applicants with black sounding names. Erza Klein. "Racism Isn't Over. But Policymakers from both Parties Like to Pretend It Is." The Washington Post. Web. 1 December 2013. < https://www.washingtonpost.com/news/wonk/wp/2013/12/01/racism-isnt-over-but-policymakers-from-both-parties-like-to-pretend-it-is/>.

6. Paul Von Zielbauer. "Race a Factor in Job Offers for Ex-Convicts." The New York Times. Web. 17 June 2005. < http://www.nytimes.com/2005/06/17/nyregion/race-a-factor-in-job-offers-for-exconvicts.html>.

7. "Freedom is the overarching theme in postwar downhome blues music. (It is a theme in prewar lyrics as well.) The large number of songs concerned with motion, journeys, and anticipation suggests that freedom is at the heart of their expression. The overt subject matter of many songs, mistreatment (and what the singer will do about it), allows the singer to express a desire for freedom more concretely." Jeff Todd Titon. Downhome Blues Lyrics: An Anthology from the Post-World War II Era. Urbana, IL: University of Illinois Press, 1990, p. 10.

8. See generally, Marcus Reeves, Somebody Scream!: Rap Music's Rise to Prominence in the Aftershock of Black Power. New York: Faber and Faber, Inc., 2008, p. 248.

9. Robert T. Tauber. Self-Fulfilling Prophecy: A Practical Guide to Its Use in Education. Westport, CT: Praeger Publishers, 1997, p. 55.

**10.** The national teacher population is 87% white and 74% female. Patrick M. Jenlink. The Struggle for Identity in Today's Schools: Cultural Recognition in a Time of Increasing Diversity. Lanham, MD: Rowman & Littlefield Publishers, Inc., 2009.

**11.** See generally Anthony J. Nocella, Priya Parmar, David Stovall. From Education to Incarceration: Dismantling the School-to-Prison Pipeline. New York: Peter Lang, 2014.

**12.** For thorough and insightful commentary on Richard Wright's genius magnus opus, see generally, James Baldwin. Notes of a Native Son. Boston, MA: Beacon Press, 1955.

**13.** Erza Klein. "Racism Isn't Over. But Policymakers from both Parties Like to Pretend It Is."

**14.** Cormega samples Isaac Hayes' "Medley: Ike's Rap III/Your Love is So Doggone Good."

**15.** See "Bio: 50 Cent." *Rolling Stone.* Web, n.d. <www.rollingstone.com/music/artists/50-cent/biography>.

**16.** "I had to hustle hard and never, ever, ever give up!" from "Hate Me Now" with Puff Daddy.

# Chapter 4 References, pp. 46-56

**1.** In 1997, Chuck D released the book "Fight the Power: Rap, Race, and Reality" wherein he stated "Every time we checked for ourselves on the news they were locking us up anyway, so the interpretation coming from Rap was a lot clearer. That's why I call Rap the Black CNN." Yusuf Jah. Fight the Power: Rap, Race, and Reality. New York: Delta, 1998, p. 256.

**2.** For more about the subversive power of social media, see "The Internet and the Erosion of the Nation-State" in Social Media and the Transformation of Interaction in Society, John P. Sahlin, ed. Hershey, PA: Information Science Reference, 2015.

**3.** Chuck Philips. "It's True: Milli Vanilli Didn't Sing: Pop Music: The Duo Could be Stripped of Its Grammy after Admitting it Lip Synched the Best-Selling 'Girl You Know It's True.'" *Los Angeles Times.* Web. 16 November 1990. <http://articles.latimes.com/1990-11-16/entertainment/ca-4894_1_milli-vanilli>.

**4.** "Many mainstream Americans have an idolatrous faith in materialism, but it is tempered by opportunities (educationally and vocationally) to build their identities on something other than their possessions or appearance. While they too are consumers, they have the option to become more than mere consumers. By contrast, many inner-city residents...cannot or will not access such opportunities. Consequently, 'meaning' gets hollowed out of their world and replaced with 'image.' In this shrunken existence, kids literally kill each other for gold chains and leather jackets." Amy L. Sherman. Restorers of Hope: Reaching the Poor in Your Community with Church-Based Ministries that Work. Eugene, OR: Wipf and Stock Publishers, 1997.

**5.** For instance, Devin the Dude breaks down the sources of his storytelling: "I'd say 60 percent is really just personal sh*t I went through; 20 percent is stuff I know about somebody who's close, or a story I heard. Ten percent is wishful thinking. And the other 10 percent is some high sh*t we just thought of." Adam Bradley, Book of Rhymes: The Poetics of Hip Hop. New York: BasicCivitas, 2009, p. 167.

**6.** Analysis conducted by the U.S. Sentencing Commission showed that black males are dealt with more harshly, receiving prison sentences nearly 20% longer than white men for similar crimes. Joe Palazzolo. "Racial Gap in Men's Sentencing." The Wall Street Journal. Web. 14 February 2013. <http://www.wsj.com/articles/SB100014241 27887324432004578304463789858002>. Contributing to this disparity were greater mandatory minimum sentences imposed for crack cocaine offenses in contrast to powder cocaine offenses at a ration of 100:1. For more information about the 100:1 crack cocaine to powder cocaine sentencing ratio, see "Planet Rock: the Story of Hip Hop and the Crack Generation" narrated by Ice-T <https://www.youtube.com/watch?v=BWKo8CLL3ks>.

**7.** One study showed that a black male charged with a drug offense who had not been in juvenile prison previously was forty-eight times more likely than a white male to be sentenced to juvenile prison, illustrating the higher probability that black males are less likely to be seen as worthy of rehabilitation but rather, worthy of incarceration. Fox Butterfield. "Racial Disparities Seen as Pervasive in Juvenile Justice." The New York Times. Web. 26 April 2000. <http://www.nytimes.com/2000/04/26/us/racial-disparities-seen-as-pervasive-in-juvenile-justice.html>.

**8.** See Jill Jonnes. South Bronx Rising: The Rise, Fall, and Resurrection of an American City. New York: Fordham University Press, 1986, p. 311.

**9.** See generally Joy DeGruy. Post Traumatic Slave Syndrome: America's Legacy of Enduring Injury and Healing. Atlanta, GA: Joy DeGruy Publications, Inc., 2005.

**10.** "By 1925 total Ku Klux Klan membership was about 4 million." Lisa Klobuchar. 1963 Birmingham Church Bombing: The Ku Klux Klan's History of Terror. Mankato, MN: Compass Point Books, 2009. "A group that reached a peak membership of five thousand members, the party not only influenced radicals from every ethnic community in the United States, it inspired marginalized and oppressed people worldwide who created Black Panther Parties." Jeffrey O.G. Ogbar. Black Power: Radical Politics and African American Identity. Baltimore, MD: The Johns Hopkins University Press, 2005, p. 189.

**11.** The "Moynihan Report" was composed by Senator Daniel Patrick Moynihan in 1965. "The Negro Family: The Case for National Action." Office of Policy Planning and Research. United States Department of Labor. March, 1965.

# Chapter 5 References, pp. 58-68

1. This point is difficult to substantively establish given its ubiquity. It is akin to documenting that "the sun is important to humans." Yet, the obvious does not go unnoticed. "The primary stories that dominate media headlines focus on just three: money, sex, and power." Keld Jensen. "Money, Sex, Power: How to Get Plenty of One." *Forbes*. Web. 7 June 2013. <http://www.forbes.com/sites/keldjensen/2013/06/07/money-sex-power-how-to-get-plenty-of-one/#2715e4857a0b60a20356778b>.

2. "Bragging and boasting....This type of content, combined with put-downs, insults, and disses against real or imaginary opponents, makes up the form known as battle rhyming." p.25 Says MC MURS "When you're a young, black male in America, you feel powerless — you feel like you don't have a voice, you're disenfranchised — so when you get the microphone, you wanna just pump yourself up. I think that's where all of the bravado comes from, where all the braggadocio comes from." p. 26. Paul Edwards. How to Rap. Chicago, IL: Chicago Review Press, 2009.

3. Which is viewed as more of a threat in the public's eye — white armed militia protesting grazing rights for other live animals or unarmed black activists protesting rights for other deceased humans — what do these contrasting scenarios say about the third prong of the Unholy Trinity, Negrophobia? Compare: Rick Bowmer. "Call for Supplies as Oregon Standoff Enters Second Week." *ABC News*. Web. 10 January 2016. <http://abcnews.go.com/US/wireStory/call-supplies-oregon-standoff-enters-week-36199170> vs. Reuters. "Maryland: 16 Protesters Arrested after Baltimore City Hall Sit In." *The New York Times*. Web. 15 October 2015. <http://www.nytimes.com/2015/10/16/us/maryland-16-protesters-arrested-after-baltimore-city-hall-sit-in.html?_r=0>.

4. The "Fortune 500" is a list of the top 500 performing American companies primarily within the private sector. As of 2015, "This year's Fortune 500 marks the 61st running of the list. In total, the Fortune 500 companies account for $12.5 trillion in revenues, $945 billion in profits, $17 trillion in market value and employ 26.8 million people worldwide." "Fortune 500." *Fortune*. Web. 2015. <http://fortune.com/fortune500/>.

5. Henry Louis Gates, Jr. The Signifying Monkey: A Theory of African American Literary Criticism. New York: Oxford University Press, 1988.

6. See the argument generally offered by Harvard linguist, Adam Bradley in Book of Rhymes.

7. See generally, Howard Gardner. Multiple Intelligences: The Theory in Practice. New York: BasicBooks, 1993.

## Chapter 6 References, pp. 70-80

1. For instance, the Brookins Institute wondered hypothetically "What would Martin Luther King Jr. think of America in 2015 if he'd lived to see his eighty-sixth birthday?" concluding that "King would be disturbed by the stubborn race gaps that remain, especially in opportunity, tarnishing the idea of the American Dream. In terms of opportunity, there are still two Americas, divided by race." The study noted that: 1) half of black Americans born poor stay poor, 2) most black middle class kids are downwardly mobile, 3) black wealth barely exists, 4) most black families headed by single parent and 5) black students attend worse schools. Richard V. Reeves and Edward Rodrigue. "Five Bleak Facts on Black Opportunity." *Brookings*. Web. 15 January 2015.

2. "Speed of Light Explained through Minecraft." *MSN*. Web. 4 November 2014. <http://www.msn.com/en-in/video/technology/speed-of-light-explained-through-minecraft/vi-AAePBIQ>.

3. Anne Moody. Coming of Age in Mississippi. New York: Bantam Dell, 1968. Contrast Anne Moody's experience with the "typical" experienced showcased by mainstream outlets such as Hollywood: Ethan Anderton. "Top 25 Best Coming of Age Movies of the Past 25 Years." *SlashFilm.com*. Web. 19 June 2015. <http://www.slashfilm.com/best-coming-of-age-movies/>. Notice how many of the "Top 25 Best" selections prominently feature non-whites.

4. "Didn't know what the cops wanted; didn't have time to ask..." Ice-T, "6'n The Mornin.'"

5. "Two debut albums that made the list are the 1967 'The Doors,' which features some of the group's most iconic songs, and 'The Miseducation of Lauryn Hill,' the breakthrough recording that fuses soul, rhythm and blues, rap and reggae." "National Recording Registry to 'Ac-Cent-Tchu-Ate the Positive.'" *Library of Congress*. Web. 25 March 2015. <http://www.loc.gov/today/pr/2015/15-041.html>.

## Chapter 7 References, pp. 82-92

1. See Alison Mitchell. "Impeachment: The Overview — Clinton Impeached; He Faces a Senate Trial, 2d in History; Vows to Do Job Till Term's 'Last Hour.'" *The New York Times*. Web. 20 December 1998. <http://www.nytimes.com/1998/12/20/us/impeachment-overview-clinton-impeached-he-faces-senate-trial-2d-history-vows-job.html?pagewanted=all>.

2. Hollywood invented misogyny, not Hip Hop. For ongoing general critiques of misogyny within mainstream society, see Lauren Tuck. "Mike Jeffries Out as Abercrombie CEO because H&M, Zara, and Forever21 Are In." *Yahoo! Style*. Web. 9 December 2014. <https://www.yahoo.com/style/the-sexiest-ad-campaigns-to-c1418142250279.html>.

3. See Fredrickson, Chapter Nine, "Negro as Beast: Southern Negrophobia at the Turn of the Century."

**4**. Such hypercriticism is almost always explained rationally through a superficially reasonable context, but yet, belies subtle assumptions based upon racially problematic narratives. These hypercriticisms often manifest themselves as "microaggressions." See generally, Derald Wing Sue. Microaggressions in Everyday Life: Race, Gender, and Sexual Orientation. Hoboken, NJ: John Wiley & Sons, Inc., 2010.

**5**. Many wax philosophically about how "money is not everything" and so on. Notice, how those who proffer such statements often are in a position where they can "afford" to say so. People in dire, abject, impoverished scenarios may not subscribe to this refrain. While money may not be "everything," it sure means something within our capitalistic economy, namely, more opportunities. See generally Chuck Collins. "The Wealthy Kids Are All Right: In a Tough Economy with Dwindling Social Supports, Children of Privilege Have a Bigger Head Start than Ever." *The American Prospect*. Web. 28 May 2013. <http://prospect.org/article/wealthy-kids-are-all-right>.

**6**. Many black males are thus frequently criticized by the mainstream as having a warped view of money and its appropriate use — one frequent area of concern is that of professional sports. See Noah Davis. "An Athlete and His Money are Soon to Part." *GQ*. Web. 2 April 2012. <http://www.gq.com/story/athletes-millionaires-bankrupt-spending>.

**7**. Former Tyco CEO Dennis Kozlowski threw a "birthday party" with company funds for his wife, complete with an ice sculpture of Michelangelo's "David" filtering chilled vodka from his centrally located protuberance — among other lavish indulgences. "Jurors See Tape of Kozlowski's Party: Prosecutors Say Half of $2M for the Birthday Party on Sardinia Came from Tyco." *CNN*. Web. 29 October 2003. <http://money.cnn.com/2003/10/28/news/companies/tyco_party/>. Play the link to the edited video if nonetheless feeling adventurous.

**8**. For sport, look up the following "white collar" financial scandals of recent memory that the mainstream perhaps may not recall: Waste Management (1998), Bernie Madoff (2008) Worldcom (2002), Lehman Brothers (2008) and the Enron (2001) scandals.

**9**. See Jessica R. Key. "Objectified...Misogyny in Hip Hop Music Continues." *New Pittsburgh Courier*. Web. 28 June 2013. <http://newpittsburghcourieronline.com/2013/06/28/objectified-misogyny-in-hip-hop-music-continues/>.

**10**. Daniel Patrick Moynihan, "The Negro Family: The Case for National Action."

**11**. Id.

## Chapter 8 References, pp. 94-104

1. "Listening to Classical Music Modulates Genes that are Responsible for Brain Functions." *ScienceDaily*. 13 March 2015. Web. <http://www.sciencedaily.com/releases/2015/03/150313083410.htm>.

2. "Hip Hop has far outlasted early predictions that it would fade and die out." Daniel White Hodge. The Soul of Hip Hop: Rims, Timbs, and a Cultural Theology. Downers Grove, IL: InterVarsity Press, 2010.

3. Talib Kweli wrote entire songs about Lauryn Hill ("Ms. Hill" <https://www.youtube.com/watch?v=tRiX-ghsZbc>) and G.U.R.U. (see Marco Polo's "G.U.R.U." feat. Talib Kweli & DJ Premier, <https://www.youtube.com/watch?v=Fdgz0QNC7GQ>) while Common composed one for Assata Shakur ("A Song for Assata," <https://www.youtube.com/watch?v=AaAMJZNi5f4>) and Skyzoo did director Spike Lee ("Spike Lee Was My Hero" feat. Talib Kweli, https://www.youtube.com/watch?v=gFGd2drY4OQ).

4. Bob Goldsborough. "Lonnie Lynn Sr. Performed on Son Common's Albums." *Chicago Tribune*. Web. 24 September 2014. <http://www.chicagotribune.com/news/ct-lonnie-lynn-obituary-met-20140924-story.html>.

5. See Appropriation Example #6 for more detail.

## Chapter 9 References, pp. 106-116

1. See http://freestatements.us.

2. While not necessarily dispositive, compare and contrast how mainstream stars Lil Wayne and Justin Bieber were treated for similar offenses: http://www.billboard.com/articles/news/1559602/justin-biebers-tour-bus-raided-for-weed vs. http://www.mtv.com/news/1538571/lil-wayne-arrested-on-drug-possession-charges/.

3. Watson, Julie. "Rapper's Delight: A Billion Dollar Industry."

4. Julie Watson. "Hip Hop: Billion-Dollar Biz." *ABC News*. Web. 24 February 2004. <http://abcnews.go.com/Business/story?id=89840>.

5. "With Barack Obama ensconced as the nation's first black president, plenty of voices in the national conversation are trumpeting America as a post-racial society -- that race matter (sic) much less than it used to, that the boundaries of race have been overcome, that racism is no longer a big problem." Lum, Lydia. "The Obama Era: A Post-Racial Society?" *Diverse Issues in Higher Education*. 25:26 (Feb 5, 2009): 14-16.

6. See Joe Nocera. "Louis Armstrong, the Real Ambassador." *The New York Times*. Web. 1 May 2015. <http://www.nytimes.com/2015/05/02/opinion/joe-nocera-louis-armstrong-the-real-ambassador.html>.

7. "During the Harlem Renaissance, just as jazz and blues began to achieve mass commercial exposure and success, numerous critics in the white media...disparaged the music and the people who wrote and performed it. For some, jazz contributed to the social disintegration endemic in American cities....They complained that its 'sensual' and 'carnal' rhythms 'ruined youth' and threatened to turn back the clock of progress for Western civilization." Harvey G. Cohen. Duke Ellington's America. Chicago: The University of Chicago Press, 2010, p. 30.

**8**. For further hard-hitting analysis, see "White Beauty Standard," pp. 63-66. F. W. Gooding, Jr. <u>You Mean, There's RACE In My Movie?</u> Silver Spring, MD: On the Reelz Press, 2007.

**9**. See Meaghan Garvey. "Q-Tip Just Gave Iggy Azalea a Hip Hop History Lesson." *Complex*. Web. 20 December 2014. <http://www.complex.com/music/2014/12/qtip-iggy-azalea-history-lesson>.

**10**. Directly related to the issues raised by Q-Tip, Azealia Banks and others, T.I. ended his partnership with the former protoge he "discovered" and produced, Iggy Azalea. Shirley Li. "T.I. Says He's No Longer Working with Iggy Azalea." *Entertainment Weekly*. Web. 17 September 2015. <http://www.ew.com/article/2015/09/17/TI-Iggy-Azalea-end-business-relationship-interview>.

**11**. Brigitte Ayaz. "No Lies!: Iggy Azalea Insists Her Butt is Real Despite Having Plastic Surgery on Her Nose and Breasts." *Life&Style Weekly*. Web. 19 August 2015. <http://www.lifeandstylemag.com/posts/iggy-azalea-plastic-surgery-67431>.

**12**. For the stuff of legend, do inspect cult classic "Starwars - Gangster Rap (original)" <https://www.youtube.com/watch?v=tEeAjy-05OI> or Supa Hot Fire and his assortment of ri-donk-u-lous-ness: <https://www.youtube.com/watch?v=WZ5CFxrsHx>.

## Chapter 10 References, pp. 118-128

**1**. Staples, Brent. "How Hip-Hop Music Lost Its Way and Betrayed Its Fans."

**2**. See Katie Little. "Meet the 'Breasturant': Sin is in at These Booming Eateries." *CNBC*. Web. 11 May 2015. <http://www.cnbc.com/2015/04/02/breastaurants-and-more-where-vice-means-booming-business.html>.

**3**. Jayne O'Donnell. "Should Business Execs Meet at Strip Clubs?" *USA Today*. Web. 22 March 2006. <http://usatoday30.usatoday.com/money/companies/management/2006-03-22-strip-clubs-usat_x.htm>.

**4**. Children are often cited as a legitimate "reason" or basis for hypercriticism or public consternation of black behavior. For a recent and public example, consider the argument offered by a "concerned mother" during Carolina Panther's starting quarterback and MVP candidate Cam Newton during the 2015 season: "A Tennessee Mom to Cam Newton: Here's What My 9-Year-Old Saw." *The Charlotte Observer*. Web. 17 November 2015. <http://www.charlotteobserver.com/opinion/article45163665.html>.

**5**. National Public Radio reports that Super Bowl XLIX of 2015 was the most watched show in the entire history of the invention called the television. Eyder Peralta. "Super Bowl XLIX Was Most Watched Show in TV History." NPR. 2 February 2015. Web. < http://www.npr.org/sections/thetwo-way/2015/02/02/383352809/super-bowl-xlix-was-most-watched-show-in-tv-history>.

**6.** During a famous "wardrobe malfunction" during Superbowl XXXVIII during 2004, Justin Timberlake sings "...and I'll have you naked by the end of this song" and at the end of his live duo with Janet Jackson, removed part of Janet's costume, unintentionally revealing part of her breast, similar to that which is revealed by a mother who chooses to breastfeed publicly while uncovered. Much ink was spilled over definitions of public decency in the aftermath. "Timberlake: Family Offended by Super Bowl." *USA Today.* Web. 5 February 2004. <http://usatoday30.usatoday.com/life/people/2004-02-05-timberlake-family-reaction_x.htm>.

**7.** See the entire clip of course or skip the remaining substance at your own risk, but the specific line cited appears around the 1:54 mark: "Who is the N*gger? - James Baldwin (clip)" <https://www.youtube.com/watch?v=L0L5fciA6AU>.

**8.** Former Merrill Lynch CEO John Thain, a company that advertises its ability to manage money wisely for its clients, admittedly spent $1,200 on a trash can. Caitlin Millat. "Canned Merrill Lynch CEO John Thain's Spending Spree Included $1,200 Trash Bin. *Daily News.* Web. 23 January 2009. <http://www.nydailynews.com/news/money/canned-merrill-lynch-ceo-john-thain-spending-spree-included-1-200-trash-bin-article-1.421589>.

**9.** See generally hit television shows such as "Yo! MTV Cribs" ("crib" is an originally black slang term for house, or residence of personal dwelling) or E!'s "Live from the Red Carpet."

**10.** Excuse the "strong language," it was inspired from Disney's own 1953 relic, "Peter Pan." Until Disney executives catch wind of the link, see if you can still catch the snippet: <https://www.youtube.com/watch?v=X69bxx2zW50>.

**11.** See John McWhorter. All about the Beat: Why Hip-Hop Can't Save Black America. New York: Gotham Books, 2008.

**12.** "If we are to honestly deal with the real issues of sexism and misogyny in hip-hop, we cannot start and stop with hip-hop. Let's challenge the industry to be responsible for the images it produces and distributes, but simultaneously deal with the far-reaching and pervasive social and cultural deficiencies America has related to the protection of women." "'Cousin Jeff': Don't Blame Hip-Hop for Society's Sexism." *CNN.* Web. 8 May 2007.

**13.** In contrast to the anti-intellectualist approach, see the work of noted scholars that see Hip Hop as a pedagogical tool to facilate effective praxis within learning communities. See Marc Lamont Hill and Emery Petchauer, eds. Schooling Hip-Hop: Expanding Hip-Hop Based Education across the Curriculum. New York: Teachers College Press, 2013.

**14.** See Kathryn Westcott. "What is Stockholm Syndrome?" *BBC News.* Web. 22 August 2013. <http://www.bbc.com/news/magazine-22447726>.

**15.** See Joseph Campbell. The Hero with a Thousand Faces. Novato, CA: New World Library, 2008.

**16.** "Whether you trace it to New York's South Bronx or the villages of West Africa, hip-hop has become the voice of a generation demanding to be heard." James McBride. "Hip Hop Planet." *National Geographic.* Web. April 2007. <http://ngm.nationalgeographic.com/2007/04/hip-hop-planet/mcbride-text>. We call this voice HIPHOPOLOGY...

# The

# Beginning...

# FOR MORE INFORMATION

For more information about racial analysis within mainstream media and other product offerings from **On the Reelz Press** visit us online at:

# www.otrpress.com

Thank you for reading *You Mean, There's GENIUS in My Hip Hop?* *You will never hear* Hip Hop *the same way again . . .*

❧ ⚜ ☙